What if you fo

If you're hanging on to
on it—just trying to find your way to the life you were made for—this deeply revealing book is for you!

What are you holding on to that has a hold on *you*?

Unwilling to give up the *one ring*, Bilbo Baggins held fast to his 'Precious'; controlled by the enemy. He thought he owned the ring, but the ring *almost owned him*. Are there unhealthy thoughts or habits in your life, repeating as if a continual cycle?

Has complacency become a veneer over old wounds?

Deep down, instinctively, you know this isn't how it's supposed to be. You need to Pivot. Choosing to make a shift, you'll change old ways of thinking; moving forward in a new and better direction. Simply put, your life will be transformed as you embrace these truths:

- Your battle wounds don't define you; they *refine* you.
- You have *all* the power you need to defeat your enemy.
- You *can* choose to Pivot, transforming your future.

"The thief comes only to steal and kill and destroy; I have come that they may have life, and have it to the full." John 10:10

It's time to draw your line in the sand!
This is your Pivot Point™

"However, as it is written: 'What no eye has seen, what no ear has heard, and what no human mind has conceived'—the things God has prepared for those who love him—" 1 Corinthians 2:8-10.

Lori Ann Thompson is an author, coach, and DFY creator who works with women of faith. Step-by-step, clients are encouraged, equipped, & empowered to boldly live out the calling God has on their lives. Past or present missionaries and pastors' wives are a special emphasis.

Pivot Point

Lori Ann Thompson

Endorsements

We all have a set of lenses we look through. It's our perception. And it's our reality. But if we're not getting the results we want, it's time to pivot. When we're willing to change our perception and align it with the One who knows us better than we know ourselves, we can not only transform our mind; we can transform our world.

Through artful metaphors and her authentic personal story, Lori Thompson takes us on a journey. She draws from J.R.R. Tolkien's writing in a creative way that unlocks the secret to walking out our God-given purpose. Lori offers tools for letting go of unhealthy thoughts and habits. These tools help us understand who we are in light of God's dreams and ultimate best for us. If you're ready to cut out the lie of "not enough" and splice in the truth of "you are a masterpiece," Lori will show you the way. Get ready for a shift. It's time for your Pivot Point.

Linda Outka,
Leadership Coach
Founder of Breakthrough Solutions, Inc.
Author of Pebbles in My Shoe: Three Steps to Breaking through Interpersonal Conflict

Pivot Point breaks you from the cycle of feeling trapped, stuck, and not knowing your purpose; propelling you into Christ directed living. Lori's stories are so relatable that I found understanding, took action, and found results. They have helped to increase my knowledge about my purpose. I'm fully directed, and can now empower more and more with light.

—April Tribe Giauque, Author of Award-Nominated Pinpoints of Light

Lori Thompson is sure to inspire, ignite, and intrigue you as she shares her story; challenging you to search deep within to find your God-inspired purpose. Sharing her personal pain-points and struggles, she will show you how to make a mindset pivot, so you are open to hearing God's voice loud and clear. The beauty behind *Pivot-Point* is being able to truly connect and relate to Lori's personal experiences all the while leaning into God's will and design for your life.

—Dr. Le'Ann Downs, President, Downs & Downs
Consulting Educational Leadership

This book is a joy to read. Lori pours her heart out, exposing personal pain that brought her to a pivot point. She has a vast knowledge of scripture and how it can apply to situations in life. This book can truly help anyone looking to go deeper into a relationship with Jesus. It was a delight to read!

—Julie Rudd, Reader

PIVOT POINT

What if you found The Secret to Everything?

Lori Ann Thompson

Printed in the United States of America

Published by Author Academy Elite
P.O. Box 43, Powell, OH 43035

 1234 Holly Springs Rd., Inman, SC 29349; loriannthompson@outlook.com: loriannthompson.com

Unless otherwise noted, Scripture quotations are taken from the *New International Version*. Biblica, 2011. *Bible Gateway*, www.biblegateway.com/versions/NewInternational-Version-NIV-Bible/

Quoted words of J. R. R. Tolkien are taken from: https://www.goodreads.com/quotes/12357-i-wish-it-need-not-have-happened-in-my-time *and* https://www.goodreads.com/quotes/140704-may-it-be-a-light-to-you-in-dark-places

Paperback: 978-1-64746-545-2
Hardback: 978-1-64746-546-9
E-book: 978-1-64746-547-6

Library of Congress Control Number: 2020919282

AUTHOR ACADEMY elite

DEDICATION

For my husband, who never complained, holding the loose ends together as I worked a full-time job and this project for over a year. I love you. You're *my person.*

For my children, who've seen the best and worst of me—I love you to the moon and back, to infinity and beyond, forever and ever. I hope you know how completely you are loved and accepted.

For the many messengers of Grace who sometimes wonder if God may have dialed the wrong number when you answered His call: You are not alone. He calls you and me to a place of deeper still, and He changes the course of our lives.

> Deep calls to deep
> in the roar of Your waterfalls;
> all Your breakers and waves
> have rolled over me.
> The LORD decrees His loving devotion by day,
> and at night His song is with me
> as a prayer to the God of my life.
> Psalm 42:-8

Finally, especially for our Heavenly Father, Christ Jesus, and the Holy Spirit, who never left me in my darkest days but patiently wooed me back to Him.

"All we have to decide is what to do with the time that is given us" — J.R.R. Tolkien.

"Open my lips, Lord, and my mouth will declare your praise" Psalm 51:15.

"Fight the good fight of the faith. Take hold of the eternal life to which you were called when you made your good confession in the presence of many witnesses" 1 Timothy 6:12.

"May it be a light to you in dark places, when all other lights go out" — J.R.R. Tolkien.

TABLE OF CONTENTS

FOREWORD

Lori Ann Thompson is someone that makes a fast impression that she is a woman of faith. We met during a thirty-day business challenge designed to take her book and business to the next level. I don't believe in chance, but direction and design. I know that there is a purpose and a meaning behind everything. God has a plan for Lori, and she felt prompted to step into it.

Whenever we do this, God blesses it, and I know each reader will be blessed by this God-inspired book. I have a huge passion for helping new faith-based business owners start their business and succeed because it is God's work, and love is doing it well.

Lori showed up for those thirty days ready to transform. Through our coaching conversations, Lori's shared her legacy, her sweet spot called *Pivot Point*. It's the point at which you draw a line in the sand, jump out of the cycle you've been stuck in, and get God-connected and directed. As Lori shared with me the ideas, my mind came alive with a visual image that would figuratively and literally bring a pivot to this book.

That's when the idea came to us. What if this book physically had a pivot built into it? The book would physically open and read like any traditional book, complete with a hero's journey feeling the pain, the fear, hitting bottom only to rise with hope.

Suddenly, physically, you would have to pivot or flip the book to work through it by applying the principals taught—a complete two-for-one book!

With energy and excitement that comes after a download from God, we began stepping into this visual idea. Immediately, a spark shown in her eyes, and soon, power added to the con-versation as she embraced the power this unexpected element would add to her book. Lori felt deeply that this was the right direction to take the book. It was different, unique, and did not fit the mold—just like Lori.

Pivot Point is Lori's testimony, told to bring you hope for a better way. She teaches that nothing changes until we do, and we can't change anything without a deep connection to the Holy Triune God. Here's the best part. Lori will take you on a healing journey to help you jump out of the cycle you are in, and become God-centered, stepping into God's call on your life.

I challenge all of you who pick up *Pivot Point* to trust that God placed this book in your hands so that you can:

- Find your way back to a God-focused life, becoming closer to Him.
- Follow Christ more closely, becoming more God-connected.
- Grow in connection with the Holy Spirit, becoming God-directed.
- This is the way to step into the call on your life, which is the glory of the Triune God.

This is your *Pivot Point*. It's the secret to all you are called to!

—Niccie Kliegl, CLC, RN
Founder of Fulfill Your Legacy at niccieklieg.com

INTRODUCTION

This book is my testimony; for women of faith everywhere, who have been through *real-life* and are ready to find *real transformation*. Like they say, 'the half has not been told,' but it's sufficient to the task. Join me on this journey of healing, hope, and encouragement as you find a new and better direction for the future ahead. Choose this day as your Pivot Point™. I believe in you!

It's early September 2020. The United States is six months deep into the effects of a worldwide pandemic. Race riots and protests have taken place in various larger cities across the country. *Politics-as-usual* is more polarizing than ever.

Are we systematically marginalizing certain groups of our fellow citizens, or are we copping to guilt-by-association? Do we fix our current governmental system, or scrap it for something totally different? Should everyone mask-up for the common good, or are we being fed a lot of hype?

Do we fully re-open schools or hybridize the educational experience? Should we be shuttering our churches as non-essential establishments, while pronouncing abortion clinics and liquor stores essential? These are some of the challenges and questions of the day. Pundits call for a pivot in the way we do business, policing, school, church, and every-day life. What then shall we do?

The book you're holding isn't the book I thought I was supposed to be writing. After six-plus months of researching, writing, mining for just the right Bible verses, or Tolkien quotes, then writing some more—something began to change.

I began to feel the message taking a turn. I tried to build a story-bridge between what I thought the book was about and what it was becoming. Confused, yet compelled to keep moving forward, I pressed on. The book proposal was already submitted and approved by my publisher. "Lord, just your words, not mine," has been my constant prayer.

I know how this will sound, but one morning, I woke up, and the phrase, 'Pivot Point,' was immediately in my head. Just like that—before there was any talk of pivots, or change, or any of the other calls for mind-shifts occupying the airspace these days. It was mid-March 2020.

As soon as *Pivot Point* entered my internal awareness, I understood the direction my book was taking. Weeks later, I began hearing everyone talk about making a pivot. I felt a pinch in my brain. *Shoot!* Just when I thought I'd been given something unique.

If God had waited just a few weeks later to plant the impression, I probably would have pushed it aside. Why? Because I've never liked doing the bandwagon thing. It goes against my grain. Wanting to follow where the Lord was taking me, I stuck with Pivot Point anyway.

I started making edits to the book I'd been writing to fit the Pivot Point theme. I contacted another author because I'd read her book and liked how her story flowed and the way she told it. We talked about my dilemma, but deep down, I already knew what was happening. She agreed. It was going to have to be a different book.

For the sake of you, the reader, it had to be the book you're holding. Two years ago, that couldn't have happened. Working through pain is a process and a road that had to be walked before sharing it. Truly miraculous healing was experienced while I searched the Bible and J. R. R. Tolkien's works for parallel truths.

Yes, with you in mind, the change was happily made; the other book, abandoned. It wouldn't have had the same impact; I'm sure of that.

What exactly *is* a Pivot Point? For our purposes, it's the point in your life when you draw a line in the sand. It's the end of the cycle you've been in. It's for those who are now where I have been, going through life on something like a roundabout. You see where you want to go but can't quite get there. Round and round you go.

Like the creature Sméagol/Gollum, who desperately longs to shed himself of the ring's curse. He and we hang on to our precious—whatever that may be for you and me. Until we say, "No more." Until we decide to make a Pivot, right here, right now, we will continue on the roundabout's circular cycle.

Yes, but how to make the shift? Simply said, we refocus on the Word so that we can reconnect with the Lord. Then He will direct our path. My story, along with snippets of familiar tales, is told to bring you hope and encouragement. I want to show you that missionaries and thieves are alike. Gurus and fast-food workers are in the same boat, spiritually speaking. Nothing changes until we do, and we can't change anything without a deep connection to and direction of our Holy Triune God.

Here's the best part. Guess what happens when you make the Pivot, get off the me-cycle, and lock arms with God? You find your way forward. You shine. You are changed, becoming—*not your best self*—but a more accurate reflection of Christ. Your life is being transformed. As a result, you become *light* to the world around you. That's life-transforming!

Finally, I want to mention one essential element implied, but not explicitly highlighted in this book. It's *Forgiveness.* The road ahead is paved with it. Without forgiveness, you'll remain at a standstill or stuck on the roundabout of your own making.

Forgive because you've been forgiven. If you're the offender, ask forgiveness, then bring the offense to the cross of Christ, so it can be flung as far away from you as the east is to the west. If you've been offended, hurt, crushed, wronged, or betrayed, forgive. Live in freedom, my friend. Choose a God-connected and directed life! It's the secret to everything.

"See I am doing a new thing! Now it springs up; do you not perceive it?" (Isaiah 43:19).

"There will be no more death' or mourning or crying or pain, for the old order of things has passed away." He who was seated on the throne said, 'I am making everything new!' Then he said, 'Write this down, for these words are trustworthy and true'" (Revelation 21:4-6).

ACKNOWLEDGEMENTS

No one travels their journey with the Lord on their own. In my case, the Holy Spirit Himself was my companion and guide. In His mercy, he brought along a few women to help me turn my face toward God, who is our source for healing. Though they may remain nameless here, they and God know who they are, and how thankful I am to have known them. They are the few who saw me through the lens of the Cross, not sitting in the seat of judgment. No, bit by bit, they lovingly flitted in and out of my life, like butterflies who bring God's glory with them wherever they go. Thank you for listening to His voice.

A huge debt of gratitude belongs to my boss-lady. Because of her generosity, I've been able to finish the work that God laid on my heart to do. The coffee shop I spent all of my Saturdays typing and researching was shut down during our present "national health concerns." I am so thankful to have had the privilege to use my work office to write nearly all of this book. Thank you for your faith and your generous spirit. You are the best example of how a lady-boss should be.

PART I

Change Your Mind

In the heart of every believer, there is an innate longing to be a part of God's plan and purpose for our lives. There's a quest to find out how we fit into the grand scheme. We are average, regular folk who have an inkling that we were made for adventure, like certain Hobbits in the tales of Tolkien. There is a nagging hunger to step out of the ordinary-ness of the shire to join forces with the One who knit us together.

Yet in the corners of our darkest tucked away places, we secretly suspect that we aren't good enough or strong enough or just enough. Because Orcs are lurking around who, in their particular disdain for Hobbits, creep out of their hiding places, eyes peeled for opportunities to destroy, they whisper lies to us we already believe, until we become quiet and complacent; happily living in our Hobbiton. Safe. But, in the words of Tolkien, "A safe fairyland is untrue to all worlds."

What if you stopped coming to the battle armed with little more than faulty beliefs? What if your perceptions of God, yourself, and the world around you were simply misinformed by your perspective? What if changing your perspective could not only win the battle but the war? What if understanding who you are in light of *whose* you are, could change everything? What if that understanding sparked a new vision, igniting a life lived on purpose, as you become more fully connected to and directed by the One who made you? What if I told you that's the secret to everything?

Chapter 1

Perception, Nine-Tenths of Reality

Wails from the deep erupted, as fountainhead gave way, giving new space to something that had been pushed down, down, *down* so I could be small and smaller still. Not wanting to rock the boat—not wanting to be disobedient, or seen as unspiritual, or unsupportive or any other descriptive words that meant I was failing at being a missionary.

I cried in anguish as the seed—planted and grown—pushed its head to the surface and made itself known. *Why? Why would He do it? Why would God give birth to a dream I'd never had and then crush me? Why would He help us conquer every obstacle to get here, and then break my heart? Why would he do that?! Why am I so alone here, and why does my husband seem indifferent to my suffering? I obeyed God's voice. I am here. Why would He allow this? I know He is sovereign. I don't understand!* My outburst of emotion and tears was a momentary release and wasn't repeated in the same context while out in the field.

In hindsight, it was probably not the best idea to ask for counsel by our missionary team member and personal friend because of our mutual employment. Can a friend and colleague offer objective, professional counsel? Is a safe space an actual possibility for the counselee? Our Member Care teammate was a licensed counselor. He and his family—who had arrived in Vienna, Austria just six months ahead of us—were also serving as missionaries. All of us were trying to figure out what our next best step was, as we wrestled with issues common to foreigners living in a new and strange-to-us culture.

Culture shock is real, painful, and can't easily be explained to those who have never stepped out of the comfort of the shire into an unknown land. Perhaps the infamous Mr. Baggins' word-picture of *feeling stretched thin, as if butter being scraped over too much bread,* would do justice.

It *would* fit the feelings of being exhausted continuously, merely trying to navigate daily life as a mom, while also wrapping your brain around the juxtaposition of adventure and opposition. Of the unexpected and overwhelming grief of leaving your just-married son and brand-new grandchild—along with your old self—back in the shire, while grasping for the new person you were supposed to be, now that you'd arrived somewhere else.

When attempting to explain it, I could only liken it to a wire coat hanger that's been twisted, stretched out, and bent unnaturally. It doesn't function the same as before. It takes on its new shape by force and can never be rightly returned to its original form or function. In the end, that can be a very good thing, but the acute pain felt in the process of contortion is intense.

I COULD ONLY LIKEN IT TO A WIRE COAT HANGER THAT'S BEEN TWISTED, STRETCHED OUT, AND BENT UNNATURALLY.

Like a hanger, I was being bent by some other force, for some other purpose. If culture shock had been the only force at play, or if I had been more adequately equipped, perhaps

I could've withstood the reshaping. Instead, I felt as if death were taking its stab at me, like the Nazgûl, who plunged its sword of death into Frodo on the mountain at Weathertop. I felt like I would never be the same. And I haven't been.

"For our struggle is not against flesh and blood, but against the rulers, against the authorities, against the powers of this dark world and against the spiritual forces of evil in the heavenly realms," Ephesians 6:12.

Much like we did—leaving behind people and places, loved and familiar—Frodo, Samwise, Merry, and Pippin left the cozy-comfort of Bag End and set out together on an adventure. Little did they know what little they knew, much like us. With a singleness of purpose, four ordinary Hobbits left the shire to be a part of something much bigger.

We four—my husband, two of our children, and I—did the same. The truth is, no matter how far your travels take you, and no matter what fellowships you may align yourselves with, you will always find you've brought yourself with you—along with more baggage than one can shoulder on the journey. So it was, with four from Bag End, and we four from South Carolina.

I've found unexpected healing and comfort in Tolkien's genius tale-telling recently. Similarities between ours and the stories of Hobbits seem to abound. Ours naturally diverges from theirs and then connects once again, here and there.

There's an old saying that possession is nine-tenths of the law. If you currently have something in your hand, the item is assumed to belong to you—unless ownership is challenged. Likewise, perception is nine-tenths of reality. At least, to the person doing the perceiving. The subjective reality, it seems, is left to the individual.

In that case, how can we know the truth of anything? While exploring the psychology of perception, I learned experiences are received in three primary ways—tactile, visual, and auditory. When events take place, we explain them in the same way. "I heard this. I saw that. I felt something here." It is what it is. Pretty simple, right? Not so much, it turns out. Let me explain.

If two people find themselves in one situation together, each one is experiencing myriad sensory information. Brains immediately go to work to process the incoming information. As witnesses or participants in a situation, the information, once processed, is formulated to explain what just took place. What if each person's perception of the same event is different from the other? Whose perception, or reality is—well—real? Perhaps there's more to it than what we perceive on the surface.

After a full year in Austria, our mission agency required us to participate in a first-year retreat, which was to gauge our emotional, relational, and ministerial health. I didn't want to go. We'd just made a quick trip back to the States to visit with my in-laws. My father-in-law was dying of cancer. I was also ever-mindful of financial scrutiny from supporters. No money was spent, it seemed, without a sideways glance cast our way to be sure we were living as spartan as possible. This was not unusual and is experienced by most missionaries.

Aside from the obvious, it wasn't the best trip home. We had limited time to speak to a few supporters and friends about our time in Vienna, up to that point. Our tales of being on the receiving end of unexpected animosity from our field director and team were met with glazed-over, wide-eyed expressions.

There was nothing in their repertoire of experience to form an understanding.

In the same way, doe-eyed expressions from my closest friends returned my gaze, as I described my then-current state of being as if I had been through a meat grinder and spat out the other side. We returned to Vienna, almost immediately piling into our car for another long trip—all the way to the resort town of Saas-Grund, Switzerland, a 14-hour drive.

Every bit of air, however wispy that previously spurred our sails onward, was now still. I'd never heard of Saas-Grund, or that Europeans consider it a skier's dream. I was broken and grieving. That was my reality. *"But Switzerland!"* you may be thinking. Yes, Switzerland. It was no vacation and wasn't meant to be, but Switzerland was the place God met me in my grief and brokenness—the first of many places he showed me His perspective, which changed my perception.

> "For now we see through a glass, darkly; but then face to face: now I know in part; but then shall I know even as also I am known" 1 Corinthians 13:12 KJV.

CHAPTER 2

PERSPECTIVE, THE OTHER TENTH

The word tithe—meaning one-tenth—is a subject that sometimes sparks debate among Christian churches today. Tithing is giving *back* to God one-tenth of all you have at your disposal and was established before Moses delivered the law. When God gave Aaron's family—known as the Levites—the priesthood's duty, He also gave them ownership and charge over all tithes and offerings. This was their inheritance.

Unlike the other eleven tribes, the Levites didn't inherit the land for cultivating and raising livestock. Remembering widows, orphans, and sojourners, God established a tithe for them as well. The Israelites regularly gave an offering too, which is anything over and above one-tenth. I would encourage you to search both the old and new testaments to learn more about how God views tithing and giving. Pray for guidance and an open heart as you study it.

Why mention tithing in a book about pivoting? As you dive in to study it, you'll find that tithing is less about money and more about *perspective*. Perspective is the lens from which we view—and informs—our perception of God, ourselves, and the world around us. Many like to call this our "truth."

What if our truth can't be relied on as *the* truth? What if our lens is clouded by abuse, betrayals, feelings of abandonment, or other wounds? What if our perception—as viewed through our cloudy perspective—is keeping us from the abundant life Jesus wants to give us?

From the beginning, we've been beguiled by the idea that we can be our own God. At the very least, we believe that *we*—not God—have our best interest at heart. This belief skews our perspective. You may think you're immune to it because you've checked off all the right boxes, assuming you've listened to God's voice over your life, but you'd be wrong. "So, if you think you are standing firm, be careful that you don't fall!" 1 Corinthians 10:12

God's Word is Truth, and His perspective is revealed in the Bible. The abundant life Jesus came to give us can be ours when lived through the crystal-clear lens of God's point of view. We were meant to live a faith-activated life, deeply connected to—and directed by—our Heavenly Father, through Christ Jesus. Often that isn't the case, however. Think about it. Many times, we hold a self-informed perspective based on changing tides and circumstances.

If God created all that is, ever was, and ever will be, how can we claim to possess the right perspective apart from God's revealed truth? God doesn't *need* anything. He is sufficient unto Himself. We, on the other hand, need God for *everything.* People talk about "the universe" as if it has a power of its own, as if all good things rain down from *it*—a created thing.

The universe, and everything in it, was established by God. In the fullness of His love, God created us and then provided everything we could ever need, including our way back to Him. How amazing is it that after all we do to show God our contempt, he wants an intimate relationship with us and pursues us for it? We should marinate in that. *Let it sink in.*

God doesn't owe us anything—even for our obedience. He gives everything to us exceedingly, abundantly out of His character and love toward us. He gives us Grace in place of punishment, exchanges beauty for ashes, and runs to meet us on the road when we're still a long way off (Luke 15:20).

For that, we should lift our voices to heaven in gratitude and praise. A lot of times, we forget. We become self-focused. Our deep-down hidden agendas come squishing out the sides as they did with our friend Frodo. As he carries on with his mission, it becomes his burden. He turns inward, sometimes lashing out. Sometimes, he takes too much on his shoulders, forgetting he isn't alone. Sometimes, he lets the enemy plant seeds that weren't meant to grow and take hold there in his heart. Like I did, on my mission field—holding on to my nine-tenths, and the other one too.

Driving to Switzerland was almost comical. At least it was to me. On a steamy, late-June day, we traveled from Vienna, Austria, passing through Graz on to Klagenfurt and then into Italy. On the way, we passed exits to places everyone wants to go to. "Oh look, kids, there's the exit to Venice! Sorry, we can't go there. Oh! Hey, there's Verona, Bergamo, and Milan! Oops, nope. Can't off-shoot there either."

We did stop at a combination petrol station/restaurant on the road running parallel to the most beautiful river I have ever seen. Driving alongside it for miles, I was in awe. It was an azure-like blue I've never seen before or since. Its beauty overwhelmed my emotions. It flowed in twisty-turny fashion and moved like it was in a hurry to get to its destination, just like us. I've tried finding paint samples or any other representing color as an example of how rich and beautiful it was. I haven't found it to this day. God showed His face to me in a river somewhere in Italy, and I thanked Him for it, silently.

Arriving in Switzerland, we drove straight to a local doctor's office. Our daughter wasn't doing well. Thankfully, it wasn't serious. Antibiotics would take care of it. For the life of me, I can't remember how we knew where to go. Mobile phones weren't nearly as sophisticated in 2008. No smartphones with Google Maps to be had. Now, where on earth were we? Oh. Yes. Saas-Grund, Switzerland.

I was so exhausted from long flights followed by a long drive; I couldn't see which end was up. I knew which end was down. That was my end. With legs wobbly and stiff from being crammed into tight spaces, I walked around our Swiss hotel, taking in the scenery. I was suddenly overwhelmed by God's beautifully crafted, glacial mountains surrounding me—another indescribably magnificent sight.

Our hotel was quaint and cozy-looking—like you'd imagine a small hotel, snuggled into a glacier-surrounded Swiss valley would look. We began to explore the nearby shops, walking down the middle of the road as if a vehicle had never passed through on it. Soon enough, we settled into our rooms. Small but comfortable. We were all spent, but feeling like maybe it wasn't going to be so bad after all. Perhaps we'd find fresh wind for our sails, and a new perspective to take back to Vienna when we left. Maybe it was just what we needed. We hoped.

The retreat was mostly how I'd expected. We began to meet new friends as we gathered for meals of local fare. Breakfast was my favorite. Euro crusty-bread rolls, with cold-cuts and cheese. Liquidy yogurt over muesli. Boiled eggs.

We first-term missionaries began to seek out friendly faces, warming up to those we felt drawn to. I suppose it was just like it would be anywhere else. Gathered by the same sending organization, we came from all over Europe. Shared experiences were more profound than those usually revealed at typical work retreats. Our connection was on a soul-level. It was a mixture of mutually experienced grief, exhaustion, bewilderment, excitement, let-down, frustration, seeking-God-in-expectation, and too many other emotions to list.

Something began to happen to me there, in the valley called Saas-Grund. First, I found out I wasn't alone. There were other families there who had known the same gas-lighting, isolation, and purposeful sabotage by their leadership team. It's an old-school tactic still employed by *some* missionary leaders. Here's the thought process: *Throw them (meaning new missionaries) in the middle of the ocean, in shark-infested waters. Don't offer assistance. Do not provide a life raft.* They will, however, isolate you and tie a juicy steak to your leg. If you aren't able to swim your way out without bleeding to death, well then, you obviously can't cut it as a missionary. You have failed to meet muster.

Without providing the novice missionary with a rule book—or some form of standard operating procedures—responses to this treatment are then measured as a gauge for whether or not the rest of the team wants to work with you. You've just sold everything you own and moved across the world. Now you're being told that the team hasn't decided whether or not to work with you. That's *a lot* to absorb.

That's what had me in sackcloth and ashes (figuratively), sobbing to our friend, the counselor, just a few months before. Sadly—and happily—I found out we weren't alone. I was relieved but also disturbed by the systemic dysfunction within our organization. I should have been just as disturbed by *our* dysfunction. I'd soon understand my perspective had been all wrong.

Like any work retreat, we attended required sessions, led by our leaders in our sending agency. Veteran and retired missionaries gave a series of talks designed to encourage first termers, reveal hidden agendas, and prepare us to go back to our field. The hoped-for result was renewed missionaries, ready to continue in language-learning and ministry. During our free time, I commiserated with my new-found kindred spirits—secretly thankful for their suffering.

I'm pretty sure they were just as grateful for mine. We relished in the confirmation that we weren't crazy—as we'd begun to suspect.

WE RELISHED IN THE CONFIRMATION THAT WE WEREN'T CRAZY—AS WE'D BEGUN TO SUSPECT.

When the time came for the afternoon session on day three, I thought, "Well, I'll go to it, but it doesn't apply to me, so it's going to be boring." The session title was "Motives for Becoming a Missionary." The first premise was that no one is entirely altruistic. No matter how pure one thinks one's motives are, they are never 100% genuine. OK—I could get on board with that. No one can be pure and without flaw, except Jesus. I completely understood that truth—onward with the easy, no-crying-during-this-session session.

And then it happened. Off to the side was a retired missionary woman who had come to assist. Here and there, she had thoughts to add, or some tidbit of wisdom learned, to pass along to us. I brushed off some of what she said as unusable advice. Then she said the word that changed my perspective and my perception.

As I said, we were discussing motives. Then the lady I never saw before—or after—said, "Some people go into the mission field to find their significance." Th-whoosh! In a split millisecond, an invisible arrow met its mark. It was so sharp, and sure, I almost felt it physically. Strangely, it wasn't her word *significance* that hit me. Somewhere between her and I, it morphed into the word *accepted.*

Instantly, the word struck me dead-on, as piercing Light shined on a memory, crouching in the corner—a tiny little memory with huge implications. Three years earlier, I'd heard a voice. It wasn't a feeling, but a statement of fact, seared on my brain while at church one Sunday morning in 2005. "You are going to Europe," said the voice in my head. Fear, joy, relief, and fear again grabbed hold of me. That time, the sure-shot carried with it a lie.

It embedded so deeply I didn't know it was there. I felt it almost imperceptibly. It said to my heart, "Finally. You are accepted," as if I'd done anything in my own power. As if I hadn't already been accepted because of Christ. At the time, I considered it no more than a gnat flying by, quickly shooed away. "Where did that come from?" "Go away, gnat." I never thought of it again until it showed up with a mirror—in a ski-town—somewhere in the Swiss Alps. Unexpectedly.

The breath left my lungs—expelled with the pain and disappointment I'd earlier voiced to our counselor, ascribing it to God. Like vapor exposed to the sun, it was gone. The answer to my cries had been reflected in a word—acceptance, which equaled works. I'd unknowingly expected God to uphold His end of the bargain, as a reward for all that was given up serving Him in Austria.

I now knew that my hidden motive was God's *earned* acceptance into service. I knew that was wrong. I knew that God's Word tells me I'm accepted because of Christ, lest any-one should boast. The Word of God is quick. It's more precise than any two-edged sword. It divides even soul and spirit. Oh, how I can testify to it! I'd thought I had pure motives. I'd thought I was listening to my Father, who said, "You're going." Perhaps I was.

We went without realizing we expected God to pay us back in a way—solely for our obedience. With that as our perspective, our perceptions caused us so much heartbreak.

Not that mistreatment didn't happen, but our view of ourselves before a Holy God was flawed. Therefore, the way we perceived all that was happening was faulty too. That makes all the difference in the world.

> "Therefore judge nothing before the appointed time; wait until the Lord comes. He will bring to light what is hidden in darkness and will expose the motives of the heart" 1 Corinthians 4:5.

CHAPTER 3

IDEOLOGY, THE WORLD WE LONG FOR

It is said that personal ideology is a complex set of internal ideals, or standards, of how life should be. This set of ideals is informed by value systems and religious beliefs, experiences, and certain assumptions held by an individual. For most of us, our personal, deeply held ideology—again, based on ideals—forms the internal model of the world we long for. Unfortunately, our standards are often not met, either by ourselves or others.

The world longed for by Tolkien was rooted in his life experiences, his love for languages, and his deeply held Christian worldview. As if a golden chord to be discovered, Tolkien's Christian ideals were discreetly woven into each story he wrote. A master composer, he illuminates providence, purpose, and the extraordinary—springing forth from ordinary—repeatedly.

Alternately endearing and terrifying were the wizards, elves, and other mystical creatures of Middle Earth. They provided the stage on which our dear Hobbits would shine. The *told-tales* of Middle Earth were often glimpsed through and around the viewpoint of usually good-natured—sometimes impish—Hobbits. Identifying *himself* as one, Tolkien's Hobbits were simply ordinary folks of no consequence, caught up in—or willingly joining—epic tales. These sagas include battles from within and without.

If you take the time to read the old and new testaments with child-like eyes, God's overarching theme of redemption is illuminated as a standing stone for all time. Unlike Peter Jackson's re-telling of Tolkien's Middle Earth and beyond, all installments are available to explore at once.

As much as we love a story of epic proportions, it makes me wonder why we've relegated children's Bible learning to tamed-down cartoon depictions on felt and flannel, or color sheets. Is it any wonder many people think of the Bible as no competition for their attention?

Imagine for a moment how little children in ancient Israel would have heard such stories. Can you see it in your mind's eye? Wide-eyed boys and girls huddled around, while fathers or rabbis told awe-inspiring stories of old. I can imagine dramatically animated demonstrations during evening meals or by a fire. Children would have said, "Abba! Tell us more! Tell us more!"

There was a sense of belonging in the teaching. The fathers had standards of how the world should be, grounded by faith in a God who'd given them an identity of their own. I remember my childhood so well as I listened to the stories. My imagination was alive with ancient history and all the miraculous happenings that went on. I may not have fully understood it, but I knew the love of Christ was the central point. I knew it was God's story, it was spectacular, and He wanted us to know it. This, of course, helped to form my personal ideology.

I didn't know he'd come for me again—*the thief.* As we stood on the precipice of our big jump into missions, my husband and I considered ourselves quite ready for the task. Though he and I had struggled for decades with the results of unresolved wounds, we determined to be obedient, believing ourselves to have side-stepped any further damage. We were naive and ignorant of our naivete. As time and trials would reveal, underlying known and unknown issues contributed to our internal struggles while on the field—making us more vulnerable to attacks on other fronts.

Sometimes I wonder if the hind-sighted mental wrestling I've done around our calling has been a bit absurd. Tolkien had it right. You—and I—have been chosen. We're all called; we followers of the One who made us. We've been equipped ahead of time with strength and heart and wits to complete the task we've been chosen for, which we find at the heart of who we are. The depth of our Maker calls to the deep in us. It is the place His finger touched at conception, meant to reveal His glory from the inside outward to the world.

TOLKIEN HAD IT RIGHT. YOU—AND I—HAVE BEEN CHOSEN. WE'RE ALL CALLED; WE FOLLOWERS OF THE ONE WHO MADE US.

We've been uniquely formed as a work of art, beautiful in our time—with a longing to join the eternal, unimaginable presence and works of God. As Christians, this is the ideal, unseen world we long for. His kingdom come and will be done; on earth as it is in Heaven.

The world, under the influence of the enemy, has a job of its own. It bumps up against our ideology, challenging all we know to be true. Oh, and sly it is. Like me, dear one, I'm sure you've experienced some things in life that have seriously collided with your personal ideology. This, for me, from within the church itself. I found that even there, the world I've longed for has not yet come.

As cracks gave way, my marriage crumbled. My ears tuned to deceptive philosophy, relying on things of this world rather than on Christ. Confusion and pain reigned over my head-space, as I questioned everything I'd thought I'd known.

All the while, I heard the hissing whispers, *"Failure. You've failed. Again. You couldn't make it, could you? Who did you think you were? And where is your faith, ha-ha-ha? You couldn't even make your marriage work. I knew I'd get you somehow. You thought you were so strong. You couldn't stand up under my yoke—no, you both stepped right into my trap. Look, the church has abandoned you. Shame, Shame! You should cower in shame. That's it. Close your heart, close your mouth, and stay right there."*

Finally, I began to cry out to God in agony of spirit. "Please, help me understand! *Help me understand!* I don't. Understand. Anything." When even listening to Christian music hurt my heart, all I could pray was that prayer, such as it was.

Was my faith even real? It was so tiny now. Mustard seed? I didn't know. Love had left me, and faith was on its heels, but one thing remained. It was hope, however shaky. Hope stayed, and as I prayed repeatedly for understanding, a strange thing began to take place. Something was different. I can't quite explain it, other than to say it was the beginning of recognition—a new perception.

It was a gradual pulling away of the covers after a restless sleep filled with nightmares. Jeremiah 19:13 says, "You will seek me and find me when you seek me with all your heart." and Psalm 34:4, "I sought the Lord, and he answered me; he delivered me from all my fears." In my heart, I'd cried out, just as in Psalm 63:1, "You, God, are my God, earnestly I seek you; I thirst for you, my whole being longs for you, in a dry and parched land where there is not water."

Eleven years have passed since grief came crashing down around me. Whether by fire or sculptor's chisel & rasp, I don't know. Parts of me were being burned up—then cut and scraped away. It's been a painful process, and fear took its turn with me. Seeping into the veins, it told me God would not have me back. To that, I reply, all Glory to God that His truth still lived in me! Not only would He have me again, but He also came for me when I couldn't get to Him on my own.

I'm not yet polished, but I feel the scrapings of the old self falling away, little by little. You and I are ever being sculpted into the image-bearer He's designed us to be. That Hope I was talking about? That was the Holy Spirit, keeping the breath of life in me. Step by tiny step, I sought my Lord. Step by step, you will find him again, too. He does not turn away from His promises. You see, this ideology we hold so dearly isn't just a way to view the world. It is *the* Way, *the* Truth, and *the* Life! I pray I never again forget.

"See to it that no one takes you captive through hollow and deceptive philosophy, which depends on human tradition and the elemental spiritual forces of this world rather than on Christ" Colossians 2:8.

CHAPTER 4
IDENTITY, WHO AM I?

Identity, it seems, can be fragile. If it weren't so, volumes written about how we can bolster ourselves and our self-image would have faded from view long ago. My own identity has proven to be just as vulnerable as the next person's, even as a Christian. Consider this truth, "But you are a chosen people, a royal priesthood, a holy nation, God's special possession, that you may declare the praises of him who called you out of darkness into his wonderful light" 1 Peter 2:9.

At the age of eight, one of my chores was ironing. I learned to sew a dress for myself and constructed a backyard clubhouse too—hammer and nails, saw, and measuring tape in hand. It seemed pretty ordinary then. Now, the thought of an eight-year-old schlepping around with a hammer and saw is cringe-worthy.

By age nine or ten, I was fiercely confident. I always felt much older than I was, having thoughts and ideas that seemed different from my peers. Hours on end were spent planning neighborhood extravaganzas, to be ticketed at $1.00 per person. My big plans never panned out. Dreaming and scheming, along with costume creation and directing the other kids—A.K.A bossing—used up the day's allotted playtime.

Each friend I'd recruited for the event was summarily dispatched back to their home, just as the streetlamp gave off its moth-attracting glow. That was the universal rule understood by all kids in the late 1960s.

I was always making something. Or drawing. I loved to draw! Reading was another favorite pastime. Many a day was spent nose-in with World Book Encyclopedias, those blue Bible-Story books, or any other book I could get my hands on. I saw myself as smart and daring enough to try most things. It was a happy childhood; until it wasn't.

MY IDENTITY'S MOORINGS HAD BEEN SCRAMBLED, LIKE CRACKED EGGS, WITH INSIDES SLIDING TO AND FRO;

One day, out of the blue-clear sky—as Forrest Gump would put it—my dad sat on the sofa, gathering the four of us together—me, my two sisters, and brother—to tell us he would soon have to find another place to live. At our mother's request. He didn't know why. He was crying—deep sobbing. It was something I'd never seen before, and my sensitive heart broke for him and me. After forty-eight years, the picture in my mind hasn't faded. The world as I knew it was shattered, and I would never view myself—or where I fit into it—the same again. My identity's moorings had been scrambled, like cracked eggs, with insides sliding to and fro; the heat of fire producing something entirely different in the end. Such are the unfortunate tales of children these days—and Hobbits.

Frodo and his companions were ignorant enough of what laid ahead when first leaving the shire. Each had their part to play and played it well. Frodo, Samwise, Merry, and Pippin were typical residents of a Hobbiton called Bag End; unassuming, but secure in who and what they were. That was until the journey toward the fires of Mordor carried them from the place their flat, hairy feet had been firmly planted—or merrily dancing, as it were. Time and life will test us all, leaving us to learn who we are deep-down and what to do with the time that's been given us. Frodo's three companions, though worn from the ordeal, returned to Bag End, living out their days better than they'd dared to dream.

Our beloved Frodo didn't fare so well. Though he seemed fair enough, a closer look revealed the troubled and distant look in his eyes. I have a suspicion. More than being pierced-through by the Witch-King's sword, Frodo's most deeply felt wound was the one inflicted by himself. The One Ring met its end—as it was meant to—though not by Frodo's hand, not altogether. He'd borne the burden. He'd gone to the edge, but just when it seemed he would complete his mission, he stopped short—leaving it to be finished by the greed-propelled mishap of a gangly creature named Gollum.

Afterward, received as a hero, Frodo was no longer the happy-go-lucky Hobbit he'd been. He'd lost a part of who he was. He'd been touched too deeply by the evil things, dimming the light he'd also known. Many times, we do the same. We forget to whom we belong when the fires get too hot, and the burdens too heavy. I also have gathered broken shards of heart in hand; head bowed in shame.

"[And the Lord said,] 'Simon, Simon, Satan has asked to sift all of you as wheat'" Luke 22:31. Even so, we can have assurance that "in all things God works for the good of those who love him, who have been called according to his purpose" Romans 8:28.

Returning unexpectedly from the mission field was out of our control. We thought we'd turned a corner in ministry and were looking forward to making headway, even as I struggled to thrive. The visas we expected had never materialized. The recession in the States dwindled our funding to dangerous lows. Our children's school was being threatened with closure by the Austrian government.

We left the mission field, feeling defeated and lost. We'd had to request financial assistance from our home church to make the return trip. We weren't supposed to be going *home* so soon. Wherever *that* was, it wasn't the plan when we'd boarded a Boeing 767 bound for Austria—two of our three kids in tow. But there we were, back on a transcontinental flight to the States.

Our eighteen months in Vienna had been roughly weathered—through speed-bump sized ups and landslide-like downs. We wondered what it could all mean. Why did we go through years of preparation, still wrestling the details out while taking the faith-leap anyway—only to pack it all away and return to no-place-called-home? Self-doubt crept in, as it does when life and plans go sideways.

Doubt in God stealthily crept in, right behind. Within a few short months of returning, our marriage was in tatters. In truth, it wasn't healthy before. Stripped of who we thought we were, we forgot *whose* we were. Instead of clinging together, we licked our wounds apart from God and each other. Leaning on *our* understanding, we didn't understand anything at all. We wallowed in bitterness and feelings of failure.

If the days of our journey there and back again were dark, darker still were the days and years after. We were as if ghosts among those we thought we knew. We were wandering in place without a place to call home. We keenly felt our insignificance among men yet failed to cling to the knowledge of how highly esteemed we were—and are—by the living God.

"See, I have refined you, though not as silver; I have tested you in the furnace of affliction," Isaiah 48:10. "I have loved you with an everlasting love; I have drawn you with unfailing kindness," Jeremiah 31:3.

As with Tolkien's short, stocky heroes, many years have passed for me. I, too, am left changed by the wounds of my own making, and those wielded by others as well. "What, then, shall we say in response to these things? If God is for us, who can be against us?" Romans 8:31.

His loving patience, grace, and mercy have restored my once-shaky faith. I know my true identity and purpose is in Christ alone. By the lamp of His Word, I can see my path. Like Paul, I know I've not *arrived*, nor finished my race, yet I do press on toward the Prize, for I have God's assurance, through Christ, by His Holy Spirit. If we are followers of Christ, our identity—everything we are or ever will be is conjoined to and in Him. "I am my beloved's, and my beloved is mine;" Song of Songs 6:3.

If you feel as if you've lost your identity and purpose, or perhaps you've not yet embraced it, don't lose hope. Take hold of your faith, tie a knot in that rope, and hang on for the ride of your life. He is faithful to his promises.

"Let us draw near to God with a sincere heart and with the full assurance that faith brings, having our hearts sprinkled to cleanse us from a guilty conscience and having our bodies washed with pure water. Let us hold unswervingly to the hope we profess, for he who promised is faithful," Hebrews 10:22-23.

PIVOT POINT

The chapters you've just read were purposely arranged according to how *we* would usually prioritize each chapter heading. This Pivot Point™ study guide introduces a better order for your consideration. Using the prompts on the following pages, I hope you'll take the time to get into God's Word for personal study.

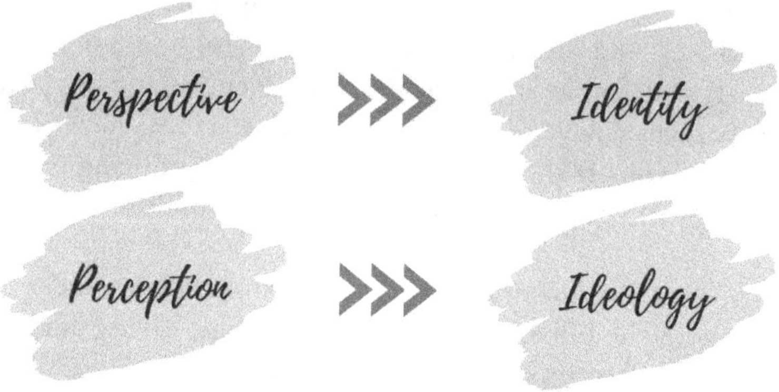

When we study and learn God's *Perspective* about who He is, and our *Identity* in Christ, our *Perception* of virtually everything is transformed, allowing us to adapt a Christ-centered *Ideology*—or worldview—for our lives.

Take a look at the following scripture references. This is just a starting point. I encourage you to search on your own for more and better clarity. A Google word-search will usually point to Bible Gateway or Bible Hub, both great study tools.

Next, use the personal notes page to journal your discoveries. Icons are provided for visual cues on what areas you'll be journaling about.

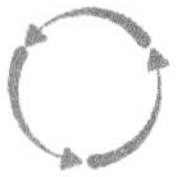

The circular icon represents the cycle of old mindsets that keeps us stuck, not relying on God's truth for life. *You'll use this area to explore areas needing improvement.*

The Bible icon is where you will write down what God has to say about a particular mindset. You'll glean that from your study of the Word.

The arrow icon represents God's direction or leading for your life based on the Biblical text. You can also think of this as your take away from scripture.

The last icon represents your Pivot Point™. The Word of God equips you to make a shift in your thinking and your direction. Give thanks to the Lord, for He is good!

The easiest way to remember what the icons represent is to think of them as The Cycle, The Word, The Way, and The Change.

Enjoy this time with the Lord, meditating on God's Word, asking the Holy Spirit to help you gain wisdom and understanding. Identify areas in your life that may need to pivot. Be willing and open to discovering God's *Perspective* about your *Identity*, which you may not have seen in the past.

Finally, friend, be in prayer for the new direction God may have for your life and praise Him for His faithfulness. He is good!

Consider studying the following Scripture:

Perspective

Isaiah 55:8-9: “For my thoughts are not your thoughts, neither are your ways, my ways, …”

Romans 3:23: “For all have sinned and fallen short…”

Revelation 3:17: “You say, ‘I am rich; I have acquired wealth and do not need a thing.’ But you do not realize…”

Identity

2 Corinthians 5:17: “Therefore, if anyone is in Christ…”

1 Corinthians 6:19-20: “…You are not your own; you were bought at a price.”

Ephesians 2:10: “For we are God’s handiwork, created in Christ Jesus to do good works…”

Perception

Romans 12:2: “Do not conform to the pattern of this world, but be transformed by the renewing of your mind…”

1 John 4:18: “There is no fear in love. But perfect love …”

2 Corinthians 12:9: “But he said to me, “My grace is sufficient for you, for my power is made perfect in weakness. …”

Ideology

2 Timothy 3:16: "All Scripture is God-Breathed…"

2 Peter 1:20: "Above all, you must understand that no prophecy of Scripture came about by the prophet's own interpretation…"

Matthew 22:36-40: "Love the Lord your God with all your heart…'Love your neighbor as yourself.'…"

Pivot Point

PART 2

Change Direction

We all face choices when joining the big adventure God has planned for us. Sooner or later, we stand at a place of turning to the left or right. We can choose the road forward or the one that loops back to where we came from; another fruitless cycle began. Forward is the direction we *want* to go, but fear can often waylay our progress. We may lose heart, frozen where we stand, going nowhere.

Similarly, Samwise Gamgee and Frodo Baggins stood at the farthest boundary of the shire, with one foot firmly planted on the soft, familiar grass they'd always known; the other, raised in combined fear and excitement. Faithful and pragmatic, Sam made a point of mentioning it, along with a warning. If you didn't *keep your feet*, there would be no telling what kind of adventure you'd be swept away with.

What if you decided to step out of *your* shire, spurred by new vision, launched by God, grounded in biblical values? What if you made a choice to walk in your fear anyway, praising God, come what may? What if you chose to believe God's perfect love is your super-power over fear? What if that was the way to overcome and choose the path forward? What if I told you these were the keys to walking arm-in-arm with God on your big adventure? What if I told you that's the secret to everything?

CHAPTER 5

VISION, THE ROAD GOES EVER ON

Chapter twenty-nine, verse eighteen of Proverbs, has been quoted throughout the centuries. It's often been misused as a rallying cry for church building campaigns, Christian organizations, and other situations necessitating vision casting. Admittedly, it was brought to mind as I began to meditate on the direction this chapter should go.

I'm sure you're familiar with the verse. The King James Version translates, "Where there is no vision, the people perish; but he that keepeth the law, happy is he." The NIV has it as, "Where there is no revelation, people cast off restraint; but blessed is the one who heeds wisdom's instruction." Commentaries seem to agree that the meaning has been largely lost to our modern vernacular. The commonly held less-than-biblical understanding was in our minds as we entered the ambiguous world of modern missions.

We caught the vision during missionary orientation with our sending agency, embracing their newly stated vision and values—especially for Austria. Not only for the Austrians but for the multi-ethnic throng in the international city of Vienna. Located in central Europe, Vienna welcomes thousands of refugees from the east. My heart was touched for this city I knew little of.

Knowing it was home to the United Nations, I was full of excitement for "the potential of the possibility of maybe" proclaiming Christ to those who'd relocated to Vienna—either sheltered or on the streets. At the time, articulating mission, vision, and values statements were a hot topic. Organizations all over the U.S. were on the bandwagon, and our sending organization was among them. Nothing out of the ordinary.

It never occurred to us to be freaked out that no assistance was offered either by our home church or sending organization on how to go about:

- Arranging for and shipping a container to a foreign country
- Navigating customs and parking permits on the street in front of our apartment
- Finding housing from thousands of miles away, before arrival
- Knowing what to consider in finding the right hous-ing location
- Enrolling our children in an international school

Among a much longer list of unknowns were:

- Which authorities had to be notified upon arrival?
- How long would it take to acquire visas?
- If no visas were forthcoming, what then?
- Aside from health and life, what kind of insurance was required?
- What would our everyday lives consist of?

- How long would it take to learn the primary language, and could we do any ministry at all—however small—while navigating that?

So many questions we didn't know to have. We must learn to accept ambiguity. That was missionary life, and the advice we'd been given at orientation. Right—every man and woman for himself. Figure it out. We were used to that. That's how our life had always rolled. After orientation, we turned our attention toward our vision casting to raise support for our project. *Ministry project* is what our family was called. This meant that we had to figure out how to get our church family and others excited about committing to pray for and financially support us in Europe. As it turned out, Europe isn't highly valued by North Americans as a mission field. More's the pity.

AS IT TURNED OUT, EUROPE ISN'T HIGHLY VALUED BY NORTH AMERICANS AS A MISSION FIELD. MORE'S THE PITY.

As we understand it, a statement of vision is a rallying cry to fight for a desired future outcome. The banner of aspirational goals is clutched, along the forward-march, by those who can envision the glorious future they see before them. Gandalf the grey—later the white—shows himself to be a wizard of higher purpose and can be seen as a masterful painter of vision himself. Who else could nudge a handful of perfectly content Hobbits out of their perfectly comfortable, child-like insular life?

Arguably depicted as an archetypical prophet in Tolkien's Return of The King, Gandalf identifies himself as a "servant of the Secret Fire" and "Imperishable Flame." Anyone who's seen the movie trilogy will well remember Peter Jackson's dramatized scene in which Gandalf infamously says, "The dark fire will not avail you, flame of Udun. Go back to the Shadow. You shall not pass!" He strikes the stone bridge with his staff, standing his ground while Frodo and his companions look on, aghast. The other-worldly power of the blow brings both Gandalf and the evil Balrog down to the depths of destruction.

Found in the Silmarillion—another of Tolkien's tomes—is the revelation of the Secret Fire, and the Imperishable Flame, of whom Gandalf serves. Fire and flame are symbolic pictures of the Creator of all things—the One we know as the Great I AM. Though Tolkien himself despised allegory, it remains for the reader to discover, nevertheless—if there is a mind to.

In the biblical sense, vision refers to prophetic vision—or a message from God to a prophet, given to the people. No self-proclaimed prophets, these are God-ordained prophets of old, chosen by El-Shaddai, God Almighty. The Israelites turned their ears to hear and know the express mandates of God. These oracles—God's standards and guidelines known as the law—were given to the people to know the way they should go.

The correct meaning of the aforementioned vision-verse would be: Where there is no prophetic word from God, the people willingly forget God's instruction. Like a woman's hair, unfurled from its tie, people cast off restraint. In doing so, they flail aimlessly with the prevailing wind, losing the peace and contentment only the Lord can provide, as they go their own way.

What then, shall we say about vision? Is our understanding without merit? Should we scrap the flawed system of understanding built around Proverbs 29:18? I would present that though we need to be careful not to ascribe to the Bible something that isn't there, we can use the understood principle. Assuming we abide in God's Word, that is.

Today, leaders, rather than prophets, inspire movement through aspirational goals—based on agreed-upon values. Thereby, an organization, group, or individual moves ahead, bringing a vision to fruition. This is *not* what some call manifestation. It is going after an end-goal by way of an individual or shared dream and then doing the work to make it happen. Without vision, we languish. We are aimless and purposeless, seeking to maintain the perceived safety of the status quo. Or worse, we perish.

In the case of our foray into Christian missions, a fresh vision was passed down by new leadership at the top of our sending agency. We grabbed hold of that vision whole-heartedly, agreeing with the values through which the image was filtered. Our aspirational goal? Be church planters. Join the team already working in Vienna. Plant churches there as part of the efforts of the Austrian Evangelical Alliance.

However, within a few short months of arrival in Vienna, several things were evident:

1. Our Viennese director and team members were not on board with the North American Office's vision.
2. We would not be connecting with the Evangelical Alliance.
3. Our on-field leadership had undisclosed plans for us, including isolating us from the rest of the team.
4. There was no vision for expanding the Kingdom amongst the *international* population of Vienna.
5. Honest questions about team evangelical efforts would be met with animosity and defensiveness.

Forbidden to participate in ministry activity of any kind until we could meet an upper-intermediate (B2) language proficiency, we were tempest-tossed, without direction. Although German is the language of Austria, English is commonly spoken in Vienna.

When I called foul to our North American agency, I was assured we'd not been sent to the field as lambs to the slaughter. Five minutes later, I received an emailed copy of my entire conversation, as sent out to missionary members on both sides of the Atlantic. I was devastated. I'd thought it had been a confidential conversation. Vision lost; I was perishing. Of course, not in the true biblical sense as in our Proverbs passage. Without vision, however, we were directionless trying to figure out why we were there.

My heart was broken, yet God showed up. Every day. He was the kindness I was compelled to extend to homeless refugees, crouched oh-so-low on Vienna's streets. He showed up in the form of students and teachers at our kids' school, and He was the Postman, delivering peanut butter and ramen noodles or yellow mustard and vanilla from the States.

The intercom buzzer would ring in our 3rd-floor apartment. Upon answering, he would cry out, "Die Post!" in a sing-song sort of way. Another day, maybe chocolate chips and pecans would arrive, along with Karo syrup, so that I could bake a pecan pie or chocolate chip cookies for our landlady. Many days I cried as the Postman handed me small packages through the locked iron gate. I looked up to the sky knowingly, as he looked at me curiously. I smiled through my tears. None of those ingredients were available in Vienna. It's always the little things, isn't it?

Even though I felt my spirit was dying, God showed up in ways only a mom could appreciate. He had a vision for me. It wasn't going to be the same vision I'd had. It wasn't going to be completed there in Vienna. My friend, He has a vision for you too. Some days it doesn't feel like it, but I know it to be true. Oh, and another thing. The pain you feel—the mess you may be sinking in—that's your mission. That's your platform. He's preparing your future steps. You can be sure of it.

> "However, as it is written: 'What no eye has seen, what no ear has heard, and what no human mind has conceived'—the things God has prepared for those who love him" 1 Corinthians 2:9.

CHAPTER 6

VALUES, WHAT'S MOST IMPORTANT?

The best way to layout aspirational goals for the future is to filter the desired outcome through a person's or an organization's deeply held values. Boundaries are created around what you do or do not participate in or allow in your space. Otherwise, it's nearly impossible to weed through the enormity of amazing things we can spend our time on. Additionally, written values help to sidestep unhealthy behaviors in ourselves or the relationships we choose to nurture. Without filtering our vision through our value system, the road we travel gets congested with weeds, distractions, and unnecessary problems. It is true for life *and* business.

Frodo's companion, Pippin, knew what his values were. Peter Jackson humorously articulates what happens when personal values bump up against corporate vision. In *The Lord of The Rings* movie, Aragorn is attempting to rally his motley group of Hobbits to continued onward movement. Suddenly, Pippin pipes up; his deeply held values are potentially compromised.

"But what about Breakfast?" he says. He is alluding to second breakfast, as he's already had one breakfast.

He goes on to further ask, "What about elevenses? Luncheon? Afternoon tea? Dinner? Supper?" It seems as if Pippin is saying, "Hey! These things are important too."

However, in the face of the greater mission, Pippin agrees to go on, with good cheer. It seems he realized the meals themselves were not the deeply held value. He valued the sense of community often shared with fellow Hobbits while eating, drinking, and making merry. We often compromise our values because of inner or outer pressure to conform to someone else's vision or value system. While this wasn't the case with Pippin, it's often a problem for us.

SOMETIMES OUR DEEPLY HELD VALUES CAN BECOME AN IDOL. WE CAN PUT THOSE VALUES, HOWEVER HONORABLE, BEFORE GOD.

Sometimes our deeply held values can become an idol. We can put those values, however honorable, before God. Ouch! I'm writing this as I wrestle with the question of whether or not I've been guilty of idolatry in a particular area of my life, or whether my feelings of conviction could, in truth, be condemnation in disguise. Satan, that serpent of old—that liar and thief—rears his fork-tongued head often enough.

One of the values I've held at the top of my shortlist is my children. Past experiences poured into my deeply held values of child-rearing. Honestly, I didn't aspire to be a career woman, or a woman who could have it all—house, home, kids, and soaring career. I wanted the picket fence, to love and be loved as in the *Song of Songs*, and to be the best mom ever. Add artist as the cherry on top. I had an idea in my head of my best life. Not surprisingly, none of that happened. However, my deeply-held values bumped up against the values held by our on-field leadership in Austria.

Within a week or two of arrival in Vienna, our director came to make a house call. During that visit, he *matter-of-factly* told me he would be looking for an Austrian family for our children to spend a week with. I met our director's statement with a pause, along with a look of confused consternation. "*Why?*" I had asked. His response was very logical, "So they can become immersed in Austrian culture right away."

My mind had started an internal dialog and checklist. Never mind, our children were attending an international Christian school, *the same as his children*. My head began to spin as he continued the conversation with my husband. My ears began to ring, drowning out most anything else that was being said. While they kept talking, the surprise directive's implications turned round and round in my head again.

My daughter was just under sixteen at the time. My son was ten—grieving the loss of friends and a sense of place. My husband had spent his career as a police officer, knowing all-too-well the dangers of letting any *rando* have access to our children. Sure, the recommended family may be fine, but what if "Uncle Hans," a closet pedophile, visited unexpectedly. What then? Also, we were reeling under all the changes taking place.

Our kids had to take a 40-minute train ride to and from school each day. We continually forgot not to buy more daily groceries than we could manage to carry half a mile. I was now being mandated to turn our children over to strangers for a week.

Voices became clearer as ringing diminished. Mama bear began to growl as the conversation turned once again to our kids and the unknown potential Austrian hosts. *"Over my dead body"* is what came out of my mouth next. "I will not give my kids over to someone I haven't had an opportunity to vet." My husband tried to smooth over the angry facial lines, now appearing on our director's face as a result of my defiance.

He brought up the potential Uncle Hans scenario, although I think he actually said Uncle Guido. Wrong country, hun. Or maybe not. I don't know where their uncle would have come from. That was the point.

Through strained facial expressions, our director told of how he and his wife had left their newborn infant with strangers to attend our mandatory annual missions conference, thirty years earlier. To which I ungraciously replied, "That was stupid." The problem we were experiencing there in our living room was a disparity of values. As expressed by our director, he thought we should be more trusting of God. "Let *God* take care of your children. *You* do what *I* say."

In my mind, God had given us the responsibility to protect our children. We did trust God. I felt that was evident in our presence in the country. My deeply held values as a mom would not allow me to acquiesce to his insistence. He backed down for the time being. Needless to say, it didn't bode well for me afterward. What stuck in my gut then, and remains now, was the suggestion that I was putting my children before God. It's a fine line, I think.

And what of you, dear reader? Have you defined your personal, deeply held values? As an exercise during pre-field training, we had to put our top 5-7 values onto paper. Married-with-children couples wrote their version of the same top three:

1. God – honor, listen, obey
2. Spouse – cherish, nurture, respect
3. Children – nurture, be an example, teach the Word

After that, there are just a few spaces available. Filling those slots can be difficult, for sure. Several things may be significant to you, but core values are non-negotiable. Those things you esteem so highly should be uncompromised. It's articulating these ideals that make our lives so much easier, though we often forget to keep the main thing the main thing, don't we?

As Christians, we can find our core values within the pages of the Bible. Some are easily visible, while other nuggets may need to be mined for. Organizational core values are a little different but can undoubtedly be scripturally based.

The endpoint is to connect your values to biblical truth. Create a self or organizational culture around those values, then filter every choice you make through those stated values. God will honor your preferences because they are aligned with His perfect will. He will light your path. All three persons of the Godhead—Father, Son, and Holy Spirit desire that we *abide* in Him. Several original-language words have been translated, abide. The root of all of them is *meno*, meaning intensive. Not a *meh* kind of word, but rich and, well—intense. A shortlist includes:

- Constant residence
- To remain or continue, instead of leaving
- To persevere
- Persistent loyalty, or continuance

My friend, you are highly valued by the Living God. Whatever you may have done or are experiencing—perhaps against your Christian values—you've been at the top of God's list. Redemption was planned for you and me at the beginning. We've been redeemed, but our spiritual maturity is an on-going process. Maturity bears fruit. Oh, that we would always abide in Him, that he would direct our paths—so we can bear faithful fruit!

"Your word is a lamp for my feet, a light on my path" Psalm 119:105.

"Abide in me, and I in you. As the branch cannot bear fruit of itself, except it abide in the vine; no more can ye, except ye abide in me. I am the vine, ye are the branches: He that abideth in me, and I in him, the same bringeth forth much fruit: for without me ye can do nothing" John 15:4-5 KJV.

CHAPTER 7

OVERCOMING, TAKE HEART, SWEET FRIEND!

Life sure can be challenging, can't it? Despite our best—and not-so-stellar—efforts to live God-centered, connected, and directed, we endure some deeply-grievous times. Jesus told us that we could take heart in knowing that He had overcome the world.

I've wondered, at times, how that could help me in the here-and-now. How could the fact that Jesus overcame help me do the same? Jesus, who is fully God, was also fully man. This is an enigmatic concept for us to absorb, isn't it?

Some think this reality gave Jesus some sort of leg-up on us, mere mortals, in the temptation department. Not so. If Jesus was fully man, he was tempted just the same as we are. The difference, I've found, is the deep connection Jesus kept with his Father. He was tempted in every way we were, yet He did not sin. Another way to say temptation is trial or testing—often felt as though we're walking through fire. Yet James tells us to consider it all joy. How can we do that?

Leaving Vienna as quickly and unexpectedly as we had was a deep disappointment; another layer, heaped upon previous ones. My journey there and back again was only the beginning. It was the beginning of another wave of gut-wrenching pain and loss. It was the beginning of crying out to God for understanding, and in the answer, the onset of understanding His heart toward us.

Tolkien's words of how an ordinary person, called a Baggins, from an ordinary place called the Shire, doing and saying unexpected things resonates, in a sense. I was carried down to the pit, and deeper still. I was looking behind rather than ahead for years, as I tried to find meaning in where I had been and how I'd arrived where I was. This, after returning from what felt like a bloody battle, because it was.

We left Vienna on January 18, 2009, having less than a month's notice for the move. Things started to get sideways in a way they never had in the past. My husband and I had a terrible fight, shooting each other with hurtful words. At the end of it, he said he was finished. He was done with our relationship. As far as he was concerned, we could just go our own way when we got back. I was hurt and in shock by his angry declaration but didn't have time to process it. The urgent is often the enemy of the most important. So, it had been throughout our marriage. I turned my attention to preparing for another international move—with no help. Again.

We arrived in the States, happy to have a temporary place to live. As we unpacked our life and feelings of loss, I tried to make our home feel like one. Our kids were resettling in their old schools. I bought some bed linens from Target for the mattress we had on the floor. I remember the hours I took, choosing just the right bed-set, making sure to keep the cost down.

Soon enough, we were able to find a used bed frame to lay them on. I'll never forget coming into our bedroom to find both king-sized beautifully shammed pillows lined up in the middle of the bed, creating a wall between one side and the other. I called it the Great Wall of China.

Several months into our cold war—after what I thought had been a "come-to-Jesus" meeting—I received an *email* from my husband, answering all of the why questions I'd asked myself and God over the past twenty years. *Why was I not good enough, or thin enough? What was I doing wrong, and how could I change? Proverbs 31; maybe that's the answer. Why was I not worthy of being loved? Why did he refuse to go to counseling with me?*

I so desperately longed to be loved by the man I'd adored. I'd finally given hope its release, after a conversation in our Viennese apartment living room. It happened somewhere between the look he'd given me—like a puppy cocking its head trying to understand your words—and the pat on the head he gave me as he walked past and continued down the hall.

There had never been true intimacy in our marriage, nor had any blossomed when I got the email. Those tightly pushed-down, hidden childhood wounds had come to collect their pay.

By keystrokes, my life and marriage were over. I was demolished completely. The guttural groans that found their way from my belly to my throat brought me to my knees. It was as if death had been thrust upon me, enveloping every part of self I ever was. Oddly, I felt liberated all at the same time. I'd been given the key to my prison door—the answer I'd been searching for—but it was too late. Days turned into weeks, and then to months as the realization sunk in that I never stood a chance.

He'd kept me at an emotional distance, to preserve his wounded inner self. Willing to offer me as a sacrifice, his childhood pain held us both hostage. Twenty-five years of my life was in a heap of ashes. I couldn't stand up under the weight of it, and I asked him to leave. The ensuing fallout left more carnage, as our church abandoned us. It was assumed

I'd done something to cause the split. Perhaps I had. Heaven knows I brought wounds of my own to our union.

Marriage is never one-sided. Still, I felt like I'd been robbed, used, laid on an altar, and I could not see my way past it. Soon afterward, I lost my job and the apartment I'd rented. Two close friends did what they could to help me financially. In the end, I ran out of cash and hope. Not a soul offered shelter—turning to their own lives and pursuits—while I left South Carolina alone, to stay with family in Michigan. My days grew darker still. Years went on before the light of day would burst through my craftily stitched canopy of pain, guilt, and shame.

Adventure is a misnomer when describing the events of Tolkien's Lord of The Rings trilogy. The fellowship of Hobbits, Elves, and Dwarves were engaged in an epic battle. Samwise, Merry, and Pippin returned to enjoy a better life than they'd hoped for at the onset. Frodo was deeply affected, but lived happily enough, for a time. No longer his former self, however, the undercurrent of experienced pain left its mark. It seems he was given extraordinary passage to convalesce with the Elves for the remainder of his days—insulated.

I suppose I could have chosen the same path. I could hide away content to lick my wounds in respite, before settling into idyllic quietude. I could also have become consumed in bitterness and anger—a perpetual victim. Or I could seek God's face, ask Him to open my eyes and give me understanding. I pivoted and chose the latter.

Jesus came to meet me where I was—sending me to family, and a few old and new friends, who unknowingly helped me begin to heal, in His time.

In 2014, after no less than four attempts, I finally landed back in South Carolina for good. It had taken three years. Meanwhile, I've remarried, and the two of us are best friends and partners. I could not have asked for a more caring person to do life with—a testimony to God's grace and mercy. It's been over a decade since I first called out to God for understanding.

I BEGAN TO REMEMBER THE THINGS I'D FORGOTTEN AND SEE THE THINGS IN MYSELF I HAD BEEN BLINDED TO.

What else could I do? I remembered Psalm 34:18, "The LORD is close to the brokenhearted and saves those who are crushed in spirit." And John 15:5, "I am the vine; you are the branches. If a man remains in me and I in him, he will bear much fruit; apart from me you can do nothing."

As for the understanding I so fervently prayed for, the Holy Spirit opened my heart's eyes once again. He applied the Balm of Gilead to my spirit. I began to remember the things I'd forgotten and see the things in myself I had been blinded to. First John 5:20 tells us, "We know also that the Son of God has come and has given us understanding, so that we may know him who is true. And we are in him who is true by being in his Son Jesus Christ. He is the true God and eternal life."

Scripture has been brought to my understanding in new ways over the past several years. It's been a long road, fraught with good and bad choices; complete with daily, relentless playback of past sins—mine and those of people in my life. Remember that the enemy is crouching low, ready to attack and devour. Take heart, and take every thought captive, friend! Don't fall for his trap of shame and lies. Christ has delivered us from our enemy, into His loving care. Our Triune God is One, in pursuit of our hearts and our praise. It's yours to *decide* to make the shift from living in a destructive cycle to a joy-filled, God-infused life of peace beyond understanding.

Every day—I mean every single day—we have to choose *this* day whom we will serve. *This* day is our Pivot Point™. He is faithful.

> "He that hath an ear, let him hear what the Spirit saith unto the churches; To him that overcometh will I give to eat of the hidden manna, and will give him a white stone, and in the stone, a new name is written, which no man knoweth saving he that receiveth it" Revelation 2:17, KJV.

CHAPTER 8

OVATION, SHOUT TO THE LORD

Ovation—a Latin-derived word meaning exult, or enthusiastic recognition is expressed in Hebrew as Halal, Yadah, Barak, Tehillah, Zamar, Shabach, and Hallelujah. All of these words boil down to what we call *praise*. In modern culture, we understand ovation and praise as relates to their secular and spiritual meaning.

We offer a standing ovation for highly skilled performances. We give our children praise for a job well done. We like to say, "Praise the Lord" a lot, here in the south. I have often found that flat sounding, even if it is heartfelt. So, let's unpack some of the renderings of ovation in the Hebrew language. In doing so, we can find richness in the meaning of ovation.

> EACH TIME I'VE SEARCHED OUT WORD MEANINGS IN HEBREW, I'VE COME AWAY FROM THE EXPERIENCE, DEEPLY TOUCHED IN MY SPIRIT.

Take a look at the bulleted list below. By no means an exhaustive list, it will expand our understanding of how the Hebrew-speaking people expressed praise to God.

- Halal: To boast or brag about God, like a raving fan. This kind of praise may make you appear foolish to a non-believer. It also means to shine brightly.
- Yadah: One meaning is to extend the hands in thanksgiving and praise.
- Barak: This means to kneel in submission, implying to bless or praise in adoration.
- Tehillah: To laud with a public song of praise—a song of adoration compelled by the attributes of God, is the meaning of this one.
- Zamar: To celebrate God with music, by way of skill on a stringed musical instrument.
- Shabach: Praise loudly as in a declaration.
- Hallelujah: This is a phrase, meaning "Praise Yah." The first part, hallelu, means to break out in a joyous song of praise (to God), with the second part, meaning our Lord. It was, at times, used as a call to worship in song. "Praise God, our Lord!"

Each time I've searched out word meanings in Hebrew, I've come away from the experience, deeply touched in my spirit. I am in awe at how vibrant the Word is and learn anew the depth of loving care our Heavenly Father has for us. The words above are written in scripture—translated as *praise*—there to shine a light on God's character and how His people expressed their deep appreciation toward Him. We are invited to do the same. He is worthy!

Witnessed through the lens of Facebook, I've watched some amazing people as they dwelt in the depths of despair. After having slowly, agonizingly lost her baby girl, Scarlett, at five months of age, a friend's daughter remained stalwart in her faith. It was a wonder to watch and strengthened the faith of many, including mine.

Another friend lost both of her daughters within two years. Still, she stands firm in her faith. That wasn't me. Not for a while—though I hadn't experienced a real death. Accustomed to dealing with life's blows on my own, the years after Vienna and my marriage's breakup were still particularly harrowing to my soul.

When walking through the valley of the shadow of death, we don't always see clearly. I remember telling people at the time; it felt like someone *had* died and that someone was *me*. There were no books to help people grieve from losses that aren't related to physical death. I looked. There was no money for a counselor, either. I knew I was grieving, yet I found little solace in the world of self-help. Some things are just not doable on our own anyway.

I hadn't been able to sit in a church service since we'd come back to the States. My heart ached with each attempt to walk into the sanctuary, and anxiety gripped me. After years of absence, I finally crossed the threshold of a church. I must have looked a sight. I cried all the way to my seat, as fear draped my shoulders like a cloak.

Little by little, I kept deciding to show up and sit in God's presence. After making my way back to South Carolina, I found a local church and started attending with my fiancé, who's now my husband. That Easter Sunday, he went forward during the altar call. I was a little confused. I thought, "Is this a rededication, or is this an *I don't think I've ever been saved* thing? It turns out; it was the latter. We both cried, and he was baptized soon afterward.

I have to tell you, without the Holy Spirit, I couldn't have chosen my pivot point—my line in the sand. With His help, I chose the better path. I made a pivot.

Not to be forsaken so quickly, the old recordings in my head played twenty-four-seven. As a natural introvert, I seem to live there—in my head. Some days it's so noisy in there, I don't even notice the radio isn't on in the car. I don't know if this happens to you, but every single day, relentlessly, the enemy brings an old sin—mine or someone's against me—to mind.

I could be thinking about something as innocuous as the flowers blooming in the yard, and there it comes, creeping in like Gollum, turning his ring end-over-end in his hands. *My precious.* Not unlike the One-Ring, this ring is a circular cycle of accusation or an old wound. It stirs up anger, jealousy, envy, strife—casting a spell-like pall over anyone paying heed to it. A soft, yet strangely compelling whisper follows, "Take every thought captive," and I am woken as if from a spell.

The past few years have proven God's faithfulness in all things. He is faithful when we aren't. He is Worthy when we show ourselves unworthy. He shelters us when we are weary. He shows up in the places we least expect, even in church. My husband and I have found a church we can call home. We belong to a *small group* we think of as an *old-fashion Sunday School class.*

There, we find food for the soul, equipped with caring warriors of prayer, at long last. The meat of the Word is served, and corporate praise is offered to the Lord. A couple of times during our time of ovation, I've felt the presence of Jesus himself. At times I sing with hands raised—closed-eyed toward heaven; unconsciously as if only I could reach high enough, I could touch the very hand of God.

One day, as I reached, I asked in the spirit for God to reach down and touch my hand. Suddenly, I had the strongest impression that Jesus was standing right in front of me, and I was stunned. The eyes of my heart—not my physical eyes—saw him. He was wearing a white robe, his arms open; hands stretched forward and opened toward me. It was as though He was saying, "I'm right here. I'm not so far away. I'm as close as I stand right now." I was overcome with emotion, tears of gratitude flowing.

Recently, I was going through multiple breast biopsies and a lumpectomy. I prayed continually, "Just the hem of your garment, Lord. Just the hem." I'd asked for prayer one Sunday, as I was scheduled that week for a biopsy with MRI.

During our worship, I stopped singing and started praying again silently, "Just the hem, Lord. Just the hem. Let me touch the hem, and all will be well." All of a sudden, I felt one of the fingers on my right-hand start to tingle like when you accidentally get an electrical shock. It lasted nearly a minute. I didn't know what to think. Later that week, I went for the MRI, which showed a small lesion on my right side, which had not been detected before. Thankfully, it was small and benign, but it makes me wonder if supernatural healing took place that day.

One thing that I know, dear friend, is ovation opens a kind of peace in your heart that wouldn't otherwise be there. It opens a new longing to know our Triune God more deeply. Every pivot we make from our old self toward the Lord is a better step than we would otherwise take.

Years ago, just before going to Austria, I wrote this ovation to God. If you're familiar with the song by Chris Rice called *Welcome to Our World,* that's the tune in my head as I wrote it:

Adopted

He has chosen
Me for His own;
am wholly
Overwhelmed.

Perfect Father
Fully blessing;
To him, I belong,
To him, I belong.

I've been wounded
He is healing;
Making beautiful
My flaws.

He is worthy
I am trusting;
Trusting in the squall.
Will I trust through all?

Patient, loving
Artfully molding;
Always faithful
Awesome God.

So I call Him
Abba, Father
Singing a new song
I'm singing a new song!©
Spring 2007

"Sing to the Lord a new song; sing to the Lord, all the earth. Sing to the Lord, praise his name; proclaim his salvation day after day. Declare his glory among the nations, his marvelous deeds among all peoples. For great is the Lord and most worthy of praise; he is to be feared above all gods. For all the gods of the nations are idols, but the Lord made the heavens" Psalm 96:1-5.

Pivot Point

Again, as in the first Pivot Point™ study sheet, consider re-ordering the way you think. Using the prompts on the following pages, I hope you'll take the time to get into God's Word for personal study.

Diving deeper into God's Word, we align our *Values* with the things of God. *Ovation*—or exuberant praise—is the result of knowing our Triune God and the depth of His loving care toward us. As a result, we begin to change our minds. Our *Vision* for the future comes into sharper focus, with new purpose. Things of the world grow strangely dim. We are *Overcoming*. Not that we've arrived, but we're getting there, step by step.

As before, use the following scripture references as your starting point. Look for more. Dig deeper into the Word. Don't forget to use the personal notes page to journal your discoveries. I would suggest the NIV or ESV as reliable translations.

The circular icon represents the cycle of old mindsets that keeps us stuck, not relying on God's truth for life. *You'll use this area to explore areas needing improvement.*

The Bible icon is where you will write down what God has to say about a particular mindset. You'll glean that from your study of the Word.

The arrow icon represents God's direction or leading for your life based on the Biblical text. You can also think of this as your take away from scripture.

The last icon represents your Pivot Point™. The Word of God equips you to make a shift in your thinking and your direction. Give thanks to the Lord, for He is good!

The easiest way to remember what the icons represent is to think of them as The Cycle, The Word, The Way, and The Change.

Enjoy this time with the Lord, meditating on God's Word, asking the Holy Spirit to help you gain wisdom and understanding. Identify areas in your life that may need to pivot. Be willing and open to discovering fresh *Vision*, inspired through *Ovation*, which you may not have seen in the past.

Finally, friend, be in prayer for new opportunities to refine and live out the calling God has on your life, as you're becoming more God-focused, connected, and directed. Give thanks to the Lord for spiritual renewal, and praise Him for His faithfulness. He is good!

Consider studying the following Scripture:

Values

Matthew 6:24: "No one can serve two masters. Either you will hate the one and love the other, or you will be devoted to…"

Luke 6:31: "Do to others as you would have them do to you."

James 1:22-27: "Do not merely listen to the word, and so deceive yourselves. Do what it says. Anyone who listens…"

Vision

Proverbs 3:5-6: "Trust in the Lord… he will make your paths straight."

Hebrews 11:1: "Now faith is confidence I what we hope for…"

Matthew 6:33: "…seek firs his kingdom and his righteousness, and all these things will be given to you as well."

Ovation

Psalm 150:1-6: "Praise the LORD. Praise God in his sanctuary; …Let everything that has breath praise the LORD."

Jude 1:25: "To the only God, our Savior, through Jesus Christ our Lord, be glory, majesty, dominion and authority, …"

Psalm 118:29: "Give thanks to the LORD, for he is good;"

Overcoming

1 Peter 5:6-7: "Humble yourselves, therefore, under God's mighty hand, that he may lift you up in due time. Cast all..."

Psalm 55:18: "He rescues me unharmed from the battle..."

1 John 5:3-4: "...for everyone born of God overcomes the world. This is the victory."

Pivot Point

PART 3

Change Your Life

Alongside the longing to join God's big adventure, there resides the love of self in the heart of every believer. Not immune to self-focused, self-aggrandizing detours along the road, we go our own way, at times. Millennia ago, the seed of doubt was planted. We cast off the perfect love of the One who made us, replacing the trust we'd known from the beginning with a lie. Even the Godliest vision, if left untethered to the Word of God, will wither as we battle Orcs within and without.

Yet in the corners of our darkest tucked away places, there is light, which penetrates the darkness of our night, bursting forth to bring a new day. It is the light of truth. It is the Truth that sets us free. Christ Jesus himself gives us a new spirit, removing our heart of stone, returning to us a heart of flesh, undivided (Ezekiel 11:19). He gives us a new name (Revelation 2:17). The whispers we once heard from the enemy are replaced with the still small voice of the Holy Spirit. *He* whispers to us; we are "fearfully and wonderfully made" (Psalm 139:14). He empowers us with the assurance that we "can do all things through Christ" (Philippians 4:13, KJV). He sets us free with the truth that in and through Christ, we are enough. He reminds us God's grace "is sufficient," because His "power is made perfect in weakness" (1 Corinthians 12: 9).

What if you came to the battle, standing your ground, confidently wearing the belt of truth, and the breastplate of righteousness? What if you fit your feet with the gospel of peace, which brings life? What if I told you the full armor of God, including the shield of faith, the helmet of salvation, and the sword of the Spirit, will not only win the battle but the entire war? What if I told you this truth would propel your vision with power to live out the call on your life, fully armed and protected by the One who made you? What if I told you that's the secret to everything?

CHAPTER 9
TRUTH,
FREEDOM IN CHRIST

Truth, it seems, is as fluid as gender these days. My truth may not be yours, and vice versa. In a world where I may *feel* like a man rather than a woman, declare myself so, *or* define myself in nebulous terms—based on an amalgamation of self-actualizing ethos—genetic truth appears to have left the room.

Many times, we're not prepared to accept the truth. Confusion reigns as many of us are left scratching our heads, wondering who cut loose our anchor. The moorings of which gave us a sense of security, based in reality. We *speak our truth* and encourage others to speak theirs. Thus, there can be no debate. Who can presume to argue with my experiential truth? No one and I can justifiably berate anyone who tries. If truth is subjective, that is.

Over time, truth—as defined in earlier generations—has become fuzzy and out of focus. We seek it, yet it eludes us. We spend our lives desperately trying to apply some bastardized form of truth to ourselves so that we can be at peace with ourselves and others.

On any given day, you can glance at your electronic device to binge-watch our confusion in real-time. Simply said, we've run amok. When faced with the choice of empirical truth or convenient truth, we downgrade to a convenient fact as long as it suits us. How can anything less be the result?

Growing up in the sixties and seventies, I was coming of age amid *sex, drugs, and Rock & Roll* culture in the United States. "Make love, not war" was spray-painted on the stop sign near my home. I remember reading it curiously, wondering what war they could be talking about. World War II had been over for some time. *Anyone* knew that. And how does one *make* love? I was 11 at the time, childishly unaware. One or two short years later, I was embarrassed within myself as I remembered the naive contemplation.

My mother never explained to us why she and my dad were getting a divorce. In those days, parents didn't feel the need to explain much to their children. Our assumed resiliency was a convenient truth bandied about in society at the time—an excuse to push limits.

Kids *are* resilient. However, just like the wire hanger I mentioned earlier, they're changed during the bending and misshaping of their lives, inexplicably altered by their parents' dysfunctional choices.

I watched my mother leave us emotionally—then altogether—while she went searching for the missing pieces of herself. Her childhood truth had been lived out in a home with a schizophrenic mom and an alcoholic, abusive dad.

Expecting me when they married, my parents were just a couple of kids hoping they'd found the one who'd fill their empty cup. My dad was content with whatever status quo they'd established, but I remember feeling the need to measure up to his standards of perfection from an early age.

And so, it goes. One generation passes their junk on to the next, leaving behind unintended carnage. I was no exception.

The truth I held close-to-the-chest was living with a husband I felt had never kept his vows. He hadn't honored or cherished me as a wife. He'd chosen self-preservation over loving intimacy. Not surprisingly, pornography had done its damage as well. To be clear, infidelity was not at issue even though it may have *felt* like it.

Our life's laundry aired; I wrongly held a belief that—contractually—I was freed from the vows I'd made. Under that belief, once separated, I didn't wait long to become friends with and then date my current husband. I felt utterly justified, conveniently. It appears my ex-husband felt the same. From his perspective, it was me—not he—who had broken vows.

He proceeded on a similar path, remarrying a few months before I did. Our children were much older than some in our situation, but later I could see lasting damage was done. I felt the weight of their disappointment, mostly in me. Shame lingered like smoke hanging over burnt, unattended dinner—unredeemable. This is not how it was *supposed* to be.

As I was enveloped in my own pain for quite some time, these revelations were slow in coming. It isn't easy seeing yourself reflected against the mirror of Truth. It never is, is it? We've all royally messed up God's best plans for us, in some way or other. It's been that way from the get-go.

God desires that we come to Him for a close intimate relationship. We were created for such a thing as this. Instead, we chase after what we think we want, missing so much that our Heavenly Father patiently waits to give us. In the beginning, God walked in a perfect garden with two perfectly created human beings.

GOD DESIRES THAT WE COME TO HIM FOR A CLOSE INTIMATE RELATIONSHIP. WE WERE CREATED FOR SUCH A THING AS THIS.

They were image-bearers of a Holy Triune God and enjoyed perfect communion with Him. Allowing themselves to be deceived, they turned away, preferring to be "like God" themselves.

When Adam and Eve believed a lie for the truth, they were instantaneously transformed. They knew their nakedness and hid from God. They covered themselves even from each other, to hide their nakedness. I don't believe this transformation took place with a dramatic gasp—the kind you'd utter when someone entered your bedroom mistakenly—as you stepped out of the shower. I believe it was a violent change.

Like innocent children, wholly trusting and unaware of themselves apart from their parents, the first humans enjoyed perfect peace and unity with their Heavenly Father. Just like that, gripping-fear entered their hearts. Mistrust in God and each other came with it. Many like to point to Eve as the culprit, who left evil's mark on us.

Adam stood by as the serpent beguiled her. Satan used his cunning against her, and she fell for it; while Adam stood by, waiting to see what would happen. Nothing is said of a change in Eve until Adam—as leader of the family—took his turn at the fruit. Once they'd both tasted spiritual death, it gripped the life from them, altering all of creation—*but God.*

God already had redemption's plan in hand as the world and all that was in it reeled. We seek after our way, turning our backs to Him. We demand explanations for troubles of our own making, at times. We who are Christians unwittingly deny His very existence by our defiance. It's time to make a Pivot.

But God—so loved us, He sent His Son to take on Himself every single deception, every evil thought or word, every narcissistic injury we've thrust upon another image-bearer. Every murder, rape, strong-armed robbery, abortion, false accusation; He said, *give them to me. I'll take them so you can be free.* We were dead in our trespasses.

- "But God demonstrates his love for us in this: While we were still sinners, Christ died for us" Romans 5:8.
- "For the wages of sin is death, but the gift of God is eternal life in Christ Jesus our Lord" Romans 6:23.
- "But God will redeem my life from the grave; he will surely take me to himself" Psalm 49:15.
- "But God chose the foolish things of the world to shame the wise; God chose the weak things of the world to shame the strong" 1 Corinthians 1:27.
- "The grass withers and the flowers fall, but the word of our God endures forever" Isaiah 40:8.

When Jesus' disciples expressed the desire to go with him wherever he was going, Jesus answered, "I am the way and the truth and the life. No one comes to the Father except through me" John 14:6.

Jesus was a truth-teller as well as a storyteller when relating to people. John R. R. Tolkien nuanced *his* writing with interlacing suggested Biblical truth. If searching for clear, unwavering truth, I'm convinced Tolkien would point his readers to Jesus all day, every day.

My friend, if you're looking for truth, you can give your life to, Jesus Christ is that truth.

1 Timothy 1:15-16 presents, "Here is a trustworthy saying that deserves full acceptance: Christ Jesus came into the world to save sinners—of whom I am the worst. But for that very reason I was shown mercy so that in me, the worst of sinners, Christ Jesus might display his immense patience as an example for those who would believe in him and receive eternal life."

"If you hold to my teaching, you are really my disciples. Then you will know the truth, and the truth will set you free" John 8:31-32.

CHAPTER 10

TRANSFORMATION, MAKING THE PIVOT

Early on—during my exile from South Carolina—I cried daily. Unemployed and laid-out with double pneumonia, I had plenty of time alone with my thoughts and replaying the previous few years. After they'd done their job, replacement thoughts were sent to bring up memories spanning my entire life. Every single day, the loop played back for me. Every day, doubts in myself and others dug in. The roots of faith, barely intact, withered.

Like an unwanted guest, my transgressions or someone else's burst into my days—lodging accusations. I wandered grocery stores weeping, not remembering what I'd come for. Months in—when I'd finally gotten a job—tears flowed freely on the way to and from work, during dinner, and before going to sleep. Grief enveloped me. It was a dark place. Hope diminished; yet, refused to leave altogether.

On the outside, I appeared to be doing oh-so-well, happy in a new life far away. At least those were the comments I received on Facebook. I put on a good front, but inside I felt completely broken—damaged goods. That's not to say that eventually, I didn't have good days. After a time, I did, while the undercurrent remained. I was traveling on the roundabout of re-cycled pain.

Through the clarity of hindsight, I see the mercy and patience God extended to me during that time. Surely, I needed a heaping helping of both. As I stumbled along ingloriously, my thoughts were berating, rather than convicting. The loop played on in my head, goading me toward the wider path. *Narrow is the way,* I heard whispered from deep within.

I gave place to my pain, practically inviting it to sit at the dinner table. All the while, I stuffed my ears with condemnation as the still small voice of the Holy Spirit began to penetrate. By His grace, He waited for me to listen, and began to do His work.

My story, unique to me, isn't altogether so. The same is true for you. We struggle with issues common to all, even if played out in various ways with varying degrees of consequences. Pain enters every life and settles like dust, which often mingles with life's carnage, becoming entrenched in our hearts' and minds' unshored cracks and crevices. Romans 7:23 tells us this, "but I see another law at work in me, waging war against the law of my mind and making me a prisoner of the law of sin at work within me."

In Peter Jackson's adaptation of Lord of The Rings, The Two Towers, we catch a glimpse—through Gollum—of the war that often rages within us. If you've seen the movie, you may notice some keywords Gollum uses against himself—the Hobbit that once was. He throws words as if poison darts, *Liar! Thief!* When that doesn't hit the mark, Gollum takes another shot with the epithet *murderer*, hoping to take down his prey. Just like our accuser does with us.

Sméagol wrestles with Gollum within and without, finally winning the battle, joyously declaring his freedom. He succumbs in the end, allowing himself to be thoroughly corrupted by his own accusatory thoughts while clinging to the only comfort he'd allowed himself to enjoy, his Precious, the destroyer of himself.

What about our thoughts? What Gollum-like battles do we allow to direct our path? We struggle within the old thought-loop that seemingly never ends. Thoughts turn to feelings of unworthiness, of being inadequate, less-than, disqualified, unqualified, or unredeemable. Abused, used, misunderstood, defeated, marginalized, set-aside, or unheard could be added to the list—and many more.

Sometimes we get confused about the messages heard within ourselves. Is it condemnation, or is it conviction? Is it God bringing us to repentance? As born-again Christians, we need not fear condemnation. Godly conviction brings about a desire to change and grow closer to God. We know, "Therefore, there is now no condemnation for those who are in Christ Jesus, because through Christ Jesus the law of the Spirit who gives life has set you free from the law of sin and death" Romans 8:1-2.

The Holy Spirit, who lives within us, pricks our conscience. He doesn't name-call or lay guilt on us, once forgiven. No, "If we confess our sins, he is faithful and just and will forgive us our sins and purify us from all unrighteousness" 1 John 1:9. We have Christ's blood-bought power to walk in freedom from guilt and shame, not living in the cycle of wrong choices based upon our old adopted names—our old identity.

How is it, then, destructive thoughts and feelings pervade our being? Often-times we fail to realize with whom we fight. "For our struggle is not against flesh and blood, but against the rulers, against the authorities, against the powers of this dark world and the spiritual forces of evil in the heavenly realms" Ephesians 6:12.

IF WE WANT FREEDOM, WE HAVE TO CHOOSE TO MAKE A PIVOT; TO LIVE TRANSFORMED, THROUGH CHRIST.

We long for change while remaining on the wide and circular path, expecting different scenery. If we want freedom, we have to choose to make a pivot; to live transformed, through Christ.

You and I *can* tear down strongholds, through the power of the Holy Spirit. We *can* take every thought—or pretension that sets itself up against the truth of God's Word—captive, bringing it and ourselves back into obedience to Christ Jesus.

We *can* refute Satan's use of our past sins against us. We have assurance—according to 1 John 4:4—that greater is He that is in us, than he that roams the world looking to kill, steal, and destroy.

We know if we are saved by grace, we have been called by the Holy Spirit. If called, then justified and glorified with Christ. "What, then, shall we say in response to these things? If God is for us, who can be against us?" Romans 8:31.

How do we fight this battle of lies, thievery, and spirit-killing brought by our enemy? We do this by nurturing and growing in a right relationship with our Heavenly Father, through Christ Jesus, with the Holy Spirit's help, who lives within us. How do we do that? We do that by going directly to the Source.

You may be asking yourself, "What if I've slipped back into some of my old ways—or worse? What if I've done things—said things? How can I get back to God from here?" I'm glad you asked, because friend, I've asked the same questions. Hallelujah!

Little by little, over time, God has been graciously teaching me through the Holy Spirit and the Word.

First, if we are in Him, God has promised never to leave or forsake us. "Let us then approach God's throne of grace with confidence, so that we may receive mercy and find grace to help us in our time of need" Hebrews 4:16. Philippians 1:6 promises that we can be "confident of this, that he who began a good work in you will carry it on to completion until the day of Christ Jesus."

No matter the depths of calamity or despair that's been allowed to enter our life, "we know that in all things God works for the good of those who love him, who have been called according to his purpose" Romans 8:28. In other words, God never wastes our pain. We may have been torn apart. It isn't for nothing. We may have been the abuser. It belongs to God, in His work for our good—and the good of others.

Whatever may have taken root in your heart that isn't of God, cut it out, and get into the Word, my friend. What an opportunity it is for you and me to intimately know the creator of the universe and all that is in it! To be able to come boldly before the throne of Almighty God, and just sit at the feet of Jesus! I don't think we still ourselves long enough to take that in.

The Bible is rich and full of the gracious, compassionate love of God. Second Timothy, 3:16-17 tells us, "All Scripture is God-breathed and is useful for teaching, rebuking, correcting and training in righteousness, so that the servant of God may be thoroughly equipped for every good work."

Make today your Pivot Point™. Choose to make the change that transforms. Refocus on a God-centered, connected, and directed life.

"Do not conform to the pattern of this world, but be transformed by the renewing of your mind. Then you will be able to test and approve what God's will is—his good, pleasing and perfect will" Romans 12:2.

"Now to him who is able to do immeasurably more than all we ask or imagine, according to his power that is at work within us, to him be glory in the church and in Christ Jesus throughout all generations, for ever and ever! Amen" Ephesians 3:20-21.

"Finally, brothers and sisters, whatever is true, whatever is noble, whatever is right, whatever is pure, whatever is lovely, whatever is admirable—if anything is excellent or praiseworthy—think about such things" Philippians 4:8.

May "The Lord bless you and keep you; the Lord make his face shine on you and be gracious to you; the Lord turn his face toward you and give you peace" Numbers 6:24-26.

Pivot Point

As Jesus preached in the synagogue to a confused crowd, He turned to those who believed in Him, and said, "If you hold to my teaching, you are really my disciples. Then you will know the truth, and the truth will set you free" John 8:31-32.

Truth >>> *Transformation*

God's *Truth* is life for us. Ultimately, God wants us to know Him by knowing the *Truth* of who He is. Jesus is the Way, the *Truth*, and the Life. Lasting *Transformation*—a changed mind, a changed direction, and life-giving purpose—can only come from God's living *Truth,* not our own understanding.

Again, use the following scripture references as your starting point. Renewing your mind through scripture will lead to *Transformation* that is lived out, as well as felt. This may happen quickly or over time. God has a purpose in the journey. It's for us to discover.

Don't worry if you don't have a significant breakthrough just now. Add your personal notes or questions to the journal section here. I would encourage you to purchase a journal, which will allow more space to reflect, pray, and offer praise for the life-change you experience as you Pivot from where you are to a fully connected & directed life!

The circular icon represents the cycle of old mindsets that keeps us stuck, not relying on God's truth for life. *You'll use this area to explore areas needing improvement.*

The Bible icon is where you will write down what God has to say about a particular mindset. You'll glean that from your study of the Word.

The arrow icon represents God's direction or leading for your life based on the Biblical text. You can also think of this as your take away from scripture.

The last icon represents your Pivot Point™. The Word of God equips you to make a shift in your thinking and your direction. Give thanks to the Lord, for He is good!

The easiest way to remember what the icons represent is to think of them as The Cycle, The Word, The Way, and The Change.

Enjoy this time with the Lord, meditating on God's Word, asking the Holy Spirit to help you gain wisdom and understanding. Identify areas in your life that may need to pivot. Be willing and open to discovering more *Transformational Truth*, which you may not have noticed in the past.

If you aren't part of a church or regular gathering of believers, be sure to do so as soon as possible. Iron sharpens iron, and we aren't meant to become islands unto ourselves. We were made for connection!

Finally, friend, be in prayer for new opportunities to refine and live out the calling God has on your life, as you are becoming more God-connected & directed. Give thanks to the Lord for spiritual renewal, and praise Him for His faithfulness. He is good!

Consider studying the following Scripture:

Trust

John 14:6: "I am the way and the truth and the life. No one comes to the Fathers except through me."

Psalm 25:5: "Guide me in you truth and teach me, for you are God my Savior, and my hope is in you all day long."

John 17:17: "Sanctify them by the truth; your word is truth."

Transformation

2 Corinthians 5:17: "Therefore, if anyone is in Christ, the new creation has come: The old has gone, the new is here!"

2 Corinthians 3:18: "And we all, who with unveiled faces contemplate the Lord's glory, are being transformed into his image with ever-increasing glory, ..."

Romans 12:1-2: "be transformed by the renewing of your mind."

Pivot Point

Pivot Point

CONCLUSION

What Then, Shall We Do?

Each journey with our Creator is as unique as the intricate way in which we're made. We are drawn by the Holy Spirit to join Him in a sacred relationship. Some of us come to Him easily, relatively unscathed by life.

Some of us have to be dragged from pillar to post and back again before deciding to consider our steps, make a pivot and change our direction—finally aware we've taken a turn in the wrong direction. Anything we do apart from Christ is futile, after all.

It's probably safe to say that you and I are kindred spirits. We've known Christ as our Savior, we've known and believed the Bible and were baptized. Perhaps our roots weren't well-fed, or *something* hadn't sunk deeply enough within the heart.

Our faith hadn't reached maturity. Though the hope within us remained, we were rocked to the core when the waves came crashing against us. Doubt and unhealthy reactions ate away at trust, which should have been growing within us.

The responsibility for our relationship with the Lord is on us. Pastors and teachers, however, bear a responsibility for leading the flock toward life-penetrating—rather than skin deep faith—which peels away like skin from your knee, at first contact with the hard places in life.

Over the past thirty-plus years, there's been a trend that's seemed harmless, even helpful. For those of us who have lived with internal messages of *not good enough, unlovable, unworthy,* or living with feelings of guilt and shame, the trend was a welcomed change.

The trend I'm talking about is the *all-about-me gospel.* It's the gospel that relegates the Great I AM, to our genie-god in the sky. God's purpose, according to the *me-gospel,* is to make you and me the center of the universe He created. We bought into that tricksy little lie.

Oh, it seemed right and sound, and uplifting. It could be entertaining. Grammy-worthy concert-style music and life-application, fireside chats have been the fare in many churches; rather than the deeper truths of the Word. The ideas of sin and eternal death aren't palatable. How can we know pure joy and devotion for our Savior if we don't fully understand what it is we're being saved from?

The *based-on so-and-so pastor* or *speaker's book* messages many received grow hollow over time, leaving unanswered questions on the side of the road, forgotten. Pastors and worship leaders became celebrities and CEOs of the church corporate. Salt lost its flavor, and light came in the form of colored beams from the rafters, flashing their message of adoration toward the stage.

Yes, it's true! *God loves us so much, He sent His only Son to die for us, taking our death-sentence upon Himself. You and I were made for a purpose.* Also true! It all points to Him, however, not us. If we shine, we shine our light toward our Heavenly Father, for others, to see. That's a life-changer!

I was steeped in the *me-gospel* culture. Subtle as a soft haze floating in on a breeze, it shrouds discernment like a veil; nearly imperceptibly. I was like the proverbial frog, who was slowly being cooked, unaware.

Oh, there were twinges of recognition here and there, but people were still being saved and baptized, so I put those twinges out of my mind. I didn't realize it until I was away from it for years; spending my time in self-imposed solitary confinement, wallowing, and reflecting; praying for God's understanding.

To be clear, I am in no way making a point against joining a church body, or against our God-ordained partnership with Him in making His name known throughout the world. "not giving up meeting together, as some are in the habit of doing, but encouraging one another—and all the more as you see the Day approaching" Hebrews 10:25. "...[Y]ou are a chosen people, a royal priesthood, a holy nation, God's special possession, that you may declare the praises of him who called you out of darkness into his wonderful light" 1 Peter 2:9.

What I am saying is we've been eating cake when we needed milk and meat. Our growth has been stunted, and we've made the *glory of us* the point of the gospel. Because of that, many of us have not been anchored by the deep, abiding faith needed to weather the storms of this life.

We look to God through our tears and brokenness, wondering why our faith hasn't *worked.* Recovery from grief, disappointment, betrayals, and even our own bad choices takes much longer than it needs to. I speak for myself, but I have a strong suspicion I'm not alone.

But God. With infinite mercy, patience, and grace, He lovingly meets us in the midst of our mess. We like to keep Him at the ready in our back pocket; but He says, "I AM."

As we get into His Word, we gain an understanding of the Trinity and begin to understand who *we* are in relationship to a Holy God. We become more deeply connected to and directed by God, through Christ Jesus, and the Holy Spirit. We make a pivot—changing our minds—changing the direction we've been traveling in, living our lives truly transformed. *(It seems I always bury the lead.)*

What then, shall we do? We allow the transformational love of God to penetrate all that we are. We re-focus on Him as the cornerstone and foundation of our lives. We find purpose in our struggle and use it as a love-offering to help others along their way.

We go out to the world, giving the love we've received, changing lives as we do. *Changed lives, change lives.* It's God who does the heart-work, but He chooses *us* to do the leg-work. Yes, He loves us faithfully. Yes, in Christ, we are worthy! Yes, there is now no condemnation for those in Christ Jesus!

You are fearfully and wonderfully made and beautiful in your time. Stand tall and confident in the Lord. Give love because you are loved.

Who deserves all of the glory for this? He does! Make today your Pivot Point™, my sister. Change your mind. Change direction. Be transformed, shining light and love to a darkened world! *It's the secret to everything.*

Day and night they never stop saying: "'Holy, holy, holy is the Lord God Almighty,' who was, and is, and is to come" Revelation 4:8.

For His glory-
Grace and Peace,

Lori Ann Thompson

Lori Ann Thompson

> Now to him who is able to do immeasurably more than all we ask or imagine, according to his power that is at work within us, to him be glory in the church and in Christ Jesus throughout all generations, for ever and ever! Amen" Ephesians 3:20-21.

Are You Ready?

It's time to make a Pivot.

This is your line in the sand!

I hope you were encouraged and spurred on in your faith as we made a Pivot together. The Flip-Side will show you the *Point* of it all.

It's the secret to everything—why you're here, what that means in your day-to-day life, and the impact you can have on the world around you.

Close the book, holding it just like you did when you first opened it. Taking hold of the sides with both hands, flip the book from bottom to top, end over end.

The Point

Is on The Flip-Side!

lori@loriannthompson.com
@heyitsme_lori
https://loriannthompson.com
https://www.facebook.com/Author.LoriAThompson

Let's do this together!

You don't have to go it alone on this journey!
Connect with me for:

- Individual Coaching
- Private Group Coaching
- Future Limited Group Retreats

the road ahead

Is waiting for you!

CPSIA information can be obtained
at www.ICGtesting.com
Printed in the USA
FSHW010946121220
76671FS

9 781647 465452

What's wrong with this book, and what's the *Flip-Side*?

Oops! If you've come here first, flip the book over to Side One. You'll want to read the author's very personal journey and how she found her Pivot Point™.

On the other hand, if you're here to move past *hanging on to hope and faith as if your life depended on it—just trying to find your way*—the Flip Side is your personal journey!

Are you ready to make *your* Pivot?

Thankfully, we are not Hobbits. As believers, you and I are image-bearers of Christ, made in the image of God. We have a sacred God-given purpose, and that purpose is to shine!

Are you willing to give up those things in life that have a hold on you?

This is your framework for getting *real and personal* with yourself and God. Our Heavenly Father is the perfect and faithful Father! His Holy Spirit will guide you as you use this tool to get God-focused, Connected & Directed, so you can live out the purpose God has for your life.

Are you ready to find true contentment, no longer living in the shadow of hidden pain?

This is how it's supposed to be! The way forward can only be found through our Triune God. Choose this day to make a Pivot. Simply put, it will transform your life.

What's the POINT of this journey?

- To help you get God-focused, bringing you closer to Him.
- With your focus on Him, you are more God-Connected.
- As your connection deepens, you are being God-Directed.
- This is the way to your purpose, which is the glory of God.

This is your Pivot Point™
Step into the transformation God has planned for your life!

"You are the light of the world. A town built on a hill cannot be hidden. In the same way, let your light shine before others, that they may see your good deeds and glorify your Father in heaven" Matthew 5:14 & 16.

Lori Ann Thompson is an author, coach, and DFY creator who works with women of faith. Step-by-step, clients are encouraged, equipped, & empowered to boldly live out the calling God has on their lives. Past or present missionaries and pastors' wives are a special emphasis.

PIVOT POINT

(The Flip-Side)

Finding The Secret To Everything

Lori Ann Thompson

Printed in the United States of America

Published by Author Academy Elite
P.O. Box 43, Powell, OH 43035

 1234 Holly Springs RD Inman, SC 29349; loriannthompson@outlook.com: loriannthompson.com

Unless otherwise noted, Scripture quotations are taken from the *New International Version*. Biblica, 2011. *Bible Gateway*, www.biblegateway.com/versions/NewInternational-Version-NIV-Bible/

Paperback: 978-1-64746-545-2
Hardback: 978-1-64746-546-9
E-book: 978-1-64746-547-6

(LCCN): 2020919282

AUTHOR ACADEMY elite

TABLE OF CONTENTS

Pivot Point

The Flip-Side

Welcome to the flip-side! Here, you'll dive in a little deeper. You'll begin to answer the question: "How do I make a pivot, and why?" Good question! The most straightforward answer to the *how* is by refocusing on the Lord as you get God-connected and directed. *How do you do that?* By getting into the Word. The *why* is so you can live out the call God has on your life. This is the abundant life. He'll show you the way.

"All Scripture is God-breathed and is useful for teaching, rebuking, correcting and training in righteousness, so that the servant of God may be thoroughly equipped for every good work" 2 Timothy 3:16-17.

The icon-key symbols are the same as in the Pivot Point™, at each section's end, on the first side of this book. This time, we will be using P.O.I.N.T. to move through the study and reflection exercises. It's my prayer that you'll experience the transformation I know God has planned for those whom He's called. As a believer and follower of the Lord Jesus Christ, you *are* called. He is yours, and you are His. His Word is Life!

"In the beginning was the Word, and the Word was with God, and the Word was God. He was with God in the beginning. Through him all things were made; without him nothing was made that has been made. In him was life, and that life was the light of all mankind" John 1:1-4. "But as it is written: 'Eye has not seen, nor ear heard, nor have entered into the heart of man the things which God has prepared for those who love Him'" 1 Corinthians 2:9.

Thus far, we've been talking about making a pivot. What's the point of a shift in our thinking or doing, unless there actually is a *point*? Another great question! The point is that we become more Christ-like.

As we become infused with the Word; remaining in prayer and forward-focused; a shift happens. It just does. You begin to see things in new light, you gain understanding, and your life takes on new purpose—to the glory of the Father—through Christ Jesus, and the indwelling of the Holy Spirit. You are living abundantly! "Do not conform to the pattern of this world, but be transformed by the renewing of your mind. Then you will be able to test and approve what God's will is—his good, pleasing and perfect will" Romans 12:2.

Let's get crack-a-lackin', shall we?

PIVOT POINT

KEY: As before:

The circular icon represents the cycle of old mindsets that keeps us stuck, not relying on God's truth for life. *You'll use this area to explore areas needing improvement.*

The Bible icon is where you will write down what God has to say about a particular mindset. You'll glean that from your study of the Word.

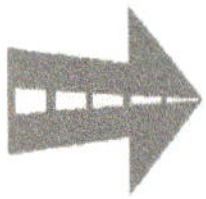

The arrow icon represents God's direction or leading for your life based on the Biblical text. You can also think of this as your take away from scripture.

The last icon represents your Pivot Point™. The Word of God equips you to make a shift in your thinking and your direction. Give thanks to the Lord, for He is good!

Remember, the easiest way to remember what the icons represent is to think of them as The Cycle, The Word, The Way, and The Change.

{P}

PRAYER, PRAISE, & PROCLAMATION

To experience life-transformation, we must renew—or change—our *minds*. I've discovered nowhere in scripture showing us how to *feel* better about ourselves or our situation *first*. Instead, we should steep ourselves in the Word of God to discern our value and God's plan for our lives.

The world confuses, but the Word of God gives clarity. Only through the clear lens of God's Word can we know God, who we are in Christ, and why we are here walking confidently in it. This is true transformation.

Consider *Prayer, Praise, and Proclamation*. These are disciplines of thought and deed, which take practice, and are our first steps toward a transformational God-connected & directed life.

Prayer

Thanks: "Rejoice always, pray continually, give thanks in all circumstances; for this is God's will for you in Christ Jesus" 1 Thessalonians 5:16-18.

Mercy:"For let us then approach God's throne of grace with confidence, so that we may receive mercy and find grace to help us in our time of need" Hebrews 4:16.

Others: "Therefore confess your sins to each other and pray for each other so that you may be healed. The prayer of a righteous person is powerful and effective" James 5:16.

Speaking from personal experience, when I have an attitude of gratitude, knowing that I can come before the throne of God—because of Christ—it makes all the difference in the world. Not only for myself. I can approach the Almighty on behalf of others as well. This time alone with our Heavenly Father brings us closer to Him and the heart of who He is. We have the promise; as we draw near to Him, He will draw near to us. Consider the scriptures above, and search for others.

With the icon-key as a guide, journal your impressions and your prayers.

Praise

Who He is: "Then I heard every creature in heaven and on earth and under the earth and on the sea, and all that is in them, saying: 'To him who sits on the throne and to the Lamb be praise and honor and glory and power, for ever and ever!'" Revelation 5:13.

Provision: "The Lord is my shepherd, I lack nothing. He makes me lie down in green pastures, he leads me beside quiet waters, he refreshes my soul" Psalm 23:1-3.

Salvation: "Praise be to the God and Father of our Lord Jesus Christ! In his great mercy, he has given us new birth into a living hope through the resurrection of Jesus Christ from the dead," 1 Peter 1:3.

Something phenomenal happens when we praise God. Our hearts are opened to the majesty of all three persons of the Trinity. As you read the scriptures provided, search out others. Recall a favorite hymn or praise song. If you're like me, you can't help but be overcome with the love of God toward us when you do this.

If you want to be genuinely moved, watch and listen (on YouTube) as Michael W. Smith sings his song, Agnus Dei—meaning Lamb of God. It slays me every time I hear it, as the holiness of the Lord washes over me. It brings to mind several men in the Bible who fell on their face when confronted with the glory of God. Yet we can approach His throne boldly. What about that?

{P} PRAYER, PRAISE, & PROCLAMATION

With the icon-key as a guide, journal your impressions and your prayers. If you're moved to do so, jot down your favorite psalm or a poem of praise to God.

Proclamation

Good News: "Day after day, in the temple courts and from house to house, they never stopped teaching and proclaiming the good news that Jesus is the Messiah" Acts 5:42.

Testimony: "However, I consider my life worth nothing to me; my only aim is to finish the race and complete the task the Lord Jesus has given me—the task of testifying to the good news of God's grace" Acts 20:24.

Jesus' Return: "Look, I am coming soon! My reward is with me, and I will give to each person according to what they have done". Revelation 22:12. "And now, dear children, continue in him, so that when he appears we may be confident and unashamed before him at his coming" 1 John 2:28. "He which testifieth these things saith, Surely I come quickly. Amen. Even so, come, Lord Jesus" Revelation 22:20.

As a young child in the nineteen-sixties, I can easily recall our preacher telling the congregation that one day every knee would bow and every tongue would confess that Jesus Christ is Lord over all. He said that one day the whole world would see Him as He is.

I wondered, with my little-girl brain, how the whole world could possibly see Him at once. It's insane the technological strides made since my childhood! Of course, we know God can make that happen supernaturally, but think of the capabilities we now have at our fi ngertips.

Until that time comes, we are left with the privilege of proclaiming the Good News to the world we come into contact

with. We do that through the reading of the Word, and through our personal story; our testimony. Jesus is coming soon!

Meanwhile, we and the heavens declare the glory of God. He will be proclaimed throughout the world. Meditate on the scripture above. Then read Psalm 19:1-14.

Write your impressions according to the icon-key.

{P} PRAYER, PRAISE, & PROCLAMATION

{O}

OMNIPOTENCE, OBEDIENCE, & OFFERING

These three are big words. *Omnipotence* means that God is all in all. He has unlimited, self-sustaining power. This is also how He is all-knowing and all-present. Our response, in light of His mighty love toward us, is *Obedience*; our life a living *Offering* to Almighty God.

All we have, we owe to our Heavenly Father. He who sent His Son as a substitute for us. Not leaving us on our own, Jesus sent the Holy Spirit to help us and comfort us. How little we give back in comparison! Not that we work our way to salvation, but we *work out* our salvation, being sanctified little by little.

Consider *Omnipotence, Obedience, and Offering*. These describe the nature of God, how we should respond, and the next steps toward transformational God-connected & directed living.

Omnipotence

All-Powerful: "'I am the Alpha and the Omega," says the Lord God, "who is, and who was, and who is to come, the Almighty'" Revelation 1:8.

All-Knowing: "Remember the former things, those of long ago; I am God, and there is no other; I am God, and there is none like me. I make known the end from the beginning, from ancient times, what is still to come" Isaiah 46:9-10.

All-Present: "Where can I go from your Spirit? Where can I flee from your presence? If I go up to the heavens, you are there; if I make my bed in the depths, you are there. If I rise on the wings of the dawn, if I settle on the far side of the sea, even there your hand will guide me, your right hand will hold me fast" Psalm 139:7-10.

When the Bible speaks of the fear of the Lord, I believe it means a very healthy dose of respectful fear. Our finite minds cannot fathom the power of our Lord. When we meditate on what the Word has to say about it, though, our *awe* should increase. Our appreciation and love should abound. Sadly, we take Him for granted too often. Let it not be so!

With the icon-key as a guide, journal your impressions, along with words of affirmation toward the Lord.

PIVOT POINT

Obedience

Our Will: "Then Jesus told his disciples, 'If anyone would come after me, let him deny himself and take up his cross and follow me'" Matthew 16:24.

Our Worship: "Therefore, I urge you, brothers and sisters, in view of God's mercy, to offer your bodies as a living sacrifice, holy and pleasing to God—this is your true and proper worship" Romans 12:1.

Our Love: "Jesus replied: 'Love the Lord your God with all your heart and with all your soul and with all your mind.'" Matthew 22:37. "My son, give me your heart and let your eyes delight in my ways," Proverbs 23:18.

This one is a tough one, isn't it? Surrendering our will, accept-ing the consequences the world may dish out as we follow Him? Yeah. We *all* struggle with that. Yet, Jesus calls us to lay everything down and follow him.

I've been watching a series called "The Chosen." In some of the behind-the-scenes bonuses, they explain what it meant in ancient Israel when a teacher—or Rabbi—asked someone to follow him. It meant the teacher would take them on as a student. The Rabbi would disciple the student, which meant shoulder-to-shoulder learning. Th at was a big deal!

It meant the Rabbi saw something in the way you were made that could be used for the greater good. Maybe you would someday become a teacher. It was an honor to *come after* the teacher, just as it is an honor for us now to surrender our will to follow after the Lord.

Our life lived in this way is our worship in love. We're pressed, then, by the power of the Holy Spirit, to love one another, as we love our Heavenly Father, through Christ.

With the icon-key as a guide, journal your thoughts. Is it difficult to be obedient to God in the ways presented here? If you're moved to do so, jot down your favorite psalm or a poem of praise to God.

{O} OMNIPOTENCE, OBEDIENCE, & OFFERING

Offering

Our Time: "Be very careful, then, how you live—not as unwise but as wise, making the most of every opportunity, because the days are evil. Therefore do not be foolish, but understand what the Lord's will is" Ephesians 5:15-17.

Our Resources: "'Bring the whole tithe into the storehouse, that there may be food in my house. Test me in this,' says the Lord Almighty, 'and see if I will not throw open the floodgates of heaven and pour out so much blessing that there will not be room enough to store it'" Malachi 3:10.

Our Life: "Whatever happens, conduct yourselves in a manner worthy of the gospel of Christ" Philippians 1:27. "In all my prayers for all of you, I always pray with joy because of your partnership in the gospel from the first day until now, being confident of this, that he who began a good work in you will carry it on to completion until the day of Christ Jesus" Philippians 1:4-6.

When we think of the word Offering, we naturally think of the basket or plate that's passed each Sunday morning. While there is some controversy over whether or not the tithe is still a mandate for today, our Offering to God can be expressed in various ways.

In gratitude, we give as God has given to us. God owns everything and gives us all we need. We're mistaken if we think we rely on ourselves for provision. Our very salvation is due to God's generosity toward us. How much more, then, shall we offer him in return?

I'll be transparent here and admit—up until recently—it's been challenging for me to give back to God in the way of

financial resources. All of my adulthood, money has been very tight. I was afraid to tithe (Oh me, of little faith!). I've now surrendered this part of my life, and it's *still scary* because the budget doesn't work out on paper. Yet, He is faithful!

The way we live, while we still have time on this earth is another way we can offer ourselves to God. We know what to do and should make good use of our time to do it; conducting ourselves in a way that shines a light on the love and character of God to those around us.

We've been created for a purpose—for God's glory. Living a life worthy of our calling is our true Offering. Meditate on the scripture above.

Are there areas that need improvement? Write your impressions according to the icon-key.

PIVOT POINT

{I}

INTENTIONAL, INTEGRITY, & ILLUMINATE

To live a life that is God-connected & directed, we do have to be intentional, don't we? We have to live life on purpose, with a purpose. We desire to exalt God, thereby reflecting illumination toward Him for others to see. We lift each other up and show others the way.

Of course, all of our intentions are fruitless if we don't walk with integrity. How many times do we hear about the hypocrisy of Christians? Mostly, this is an excuse people use to thwart personal responsibility toward God. However, let's not be a stumbling block for others to trip over.

No, instead, let's do our best to live in a continual spirit of integrity. In this way, our words and deeds will be upright before those who are watching. Do we fall short? We do! Yet, we know we can, in integrity, admit our mistakes, ask forgiveness with humility, and continue our walk in confidence.

Consider *Intentional, Integrity, and Illuminate.* These all require continual practice, in prayer, and are an essential step toward a transformational God-connected & directed Life.

Intentional

Seeking: "So I say to you: Ask and it will be given to you; seek and you will find; knock and the door will be opened to you" Luke 11:9.

Listening: "Here I am! I stand at the door and knock. If anyone hears my voice and opens the door, I will come in and eat with that person, and they with me" Revelation 3:20.

Fulfilling: "For we are God's handiwork, created in Christ Jesus to do good works, which God prepared in advance for us to do" Ephesians 2:10.

Aside from right now, the most Intentional I have ever been was during our push to get to the mission field. I was single-minded, feeling more connected to God than ever before. It's incredible how that works. The more attuned we are to *Seeking, Listening, and Fulfilling* all that God has for us, the more intentional we become.

Consider the scriptures above, and search for others. With the icon-key as a guide, pray for and journal God's leading for an Intentional life.

Integrity

In Spirit: "The integrity of the upright guides them, but the unfaithful are destroyed by their duplicity" Proverbs 11:3.

In Word: "Do not let any unwholesome talk come out of your mouths, but only what is helpful for building others up according to their needs, that it may benefit those who listen" Ephesians 4:29.

In Actions: "In everything set them an example by doing what is good. In your teaching show integrity, seriousness and soundness of speech that cannot be condemned, so that those who oppose you may be ashamed because they have nothing bad to say about us" Titus 2:7-8.

This is where the rubber meets the road, isn't it? Let's admit we fall short at times. Sometimes we fall very short. In Romans 7:15, the apostle Paul says it this way, "I do not understand what I do. For what I want to do I do not do, but what I hate I do." It seems we're in good company.

Many times, we let our old nature take precedence, over-riding our convictions. I know I've been guilty of it. There have been times I let my pain give me a license for what I knew to be deplorable in the sight of God.

Praise the Lord for the Holy Spirit, who, in His loving kindness, convicts us and brings us back to Him. This is how we live in Integrity. Not by our power but by the power of the Holy Spirit working within us. I often think that God allows failings in our lives so that we don't puff ourselves up with lofty ideas of ourselves. We know full well how far from God we can get. Thank you, Jesus, for your correction!

{I} INTENIONAL, INTEGRITY, & ILLUMINATE

With the icon-key as a guide, journal your impressions. Pray that the Holy Spirit will bring to mind those areas of Integrity that need shoring up. Ask forgiveness where there's been a shortcoming, and ask for help moving forward. We are a work in progress, my friend!

Illuminate

God: "But you are a chosen people, a royal priesthood, a holy nation, God's special possession, that you may declare the praises of him who called you out of darkness into his wonderful light" 1 Peter 2:9.

Others: "Therefore encourage one another and build each other up, just as in fact you are doing" 1 Thessalonians 5:11. "Honor one another above yourselves" Romans 12:10.

The Way: "I am the light of the world. Whoever follows me will never walk in darkness, but will have the light of life" John 8:12. "In the same way, let your light shine before others, that they may see your good deeds and glorify your Father in heaven" Matthew 5:16.

What a gift and privilege it is to be able to shine a light on who God is! I don't know if you enjoy the spotlight, or if you're like me and would rather be in the background, but we've been made to shine. Not for our glory, but God's.

"The heavens declare the glory of God; the skies proclaim the work of his hands. Day after day they pour forth speech; night after night they reveal knowledge. They have no speech, they use no words; no sound is heard from them. Yet their voice goes out into all the earth, their words to the ends of the world" Psalm 19:1-4.

Even so, *we* were made to Illuminate. He called us out of darkness to be a light. We are called to lift each other up and help each other shine. We are called to show the Way to eternal life through Christ Jesus. Not for ours, but for *His* glory.

These things are good to remember, for those of us who shy from the spotlight. He will be proclaimed throughout the world. Even if we were to remain silent, the rocks would still cry out! (Luke 19:40).

Meditate on the scriptures above. Then read Luke 19:28-40. Write your impressions according to the icon-key.

{N}

NOURISH, NURTURE, & NESTLE

Now we're beginning to make the Pivot. We're turning the corner. We see things with new eyes. Let's bask in the presence of Almighty God, who is our inheritance. These three words were impressed upon me as I sought God's leading for this letter-N-chapter. Can you feel yourself sinking into them? I can.

We're nourished by our good and perfect Father. We're free to nurture a close relationship to Him through Christ Jesus, nestling into the hope we have for an abundant life and future by the Holy Spirit. This is the joy of our salvation!

Consider *Nourish, Nurture, and Nestle*. These three are the benefits and responsibilities of remaining in transformed, God-connected & directed living.

Nourish

Bread: "Then Jesus declared, 'I am the bread of life. Whoever comes to me will never go hungry, and whoever believes in me will never be thirsty'" John 6:35.

Milk & Meat: "I fed you with milk, not solid food, for you were not ready for it" 1 Corinthians 3:2. "But solid food is for the mature, for those who have their powers of discernment trained by constant practice to distinguish good from evil" Hebrews 5:14.

Water: "If anyone is thirsty, let him come to Me and drink. He who believes in Me, as the Scripture said, 'From his innermost being will flow rivers of living water" John 7:37-38.

I wonder how often we truly meditate on the nourishment that is shrouded here in metaphorical language. Jesus used this form of communication often. Anyone who had an *ear to hear* and understand would have known His meaning.

Those who didn't thought it was merely foolish talk of another come-lately itinerate teacher. Can you imagine sitting at the feet of Jesus, taking in the *bread of life*? Think of what a good parent and friend He is to feed us first milk and then meat as we grow. And, who but the Lord, can bring forth in us a well-spring of Living Water?

Let the scriptures wash over you. With the icon-key as a guide, journal your impressions and your prayers of gratitude for His infinitely good provision.

Nurture

Follow: "It is the Lord your God you must follow, and him you must revere. Keep his commands and obey him; serve him and hold fast to him" Deuteronomy 13:4.

Abide: "Remain in me, as I also remain in you. No branch can bear fruit by itself; it must remain in the vine. Neither can you bear fruit unless you remain in me" John 15:4.

Run: "but those who hope in the Lord will renew their strength. They will soar on wings like eagles; they will run and not grow weary, they will walk and not be faint" Isaiah 40:31. "I run in the path of your commands, for you have broadened my understanding" Psalm 119:32.

Every intimate relationship needs to be nurtured. If you want closeness with your spouse or your children, you have to spend time knowing them, and they knowing you. It takes a commitment, and let's face it; it can be work. The rewards, however, are healthy loving relationships with all of the benefits that brings.

So it is with our relationship to our Heavenly Father. Deuteronomy 12:4 not only tells us to follow and obey but to *hold fast*. Think of that. When your son or daughter took hold of you as if they would never let go, you could feel that everlasting parent-child bond.

Likewise, when we nurture our connection to Christ, we can bear fruit. For fruit to grow, the branch must remain connected to the vine. Then it receives all it needs. Depending on the Lord for all of our needs—nurturing our relationship by abiding in Him—we can run the race set before us. That

is, the excellent work he has prepared for us to do. We live out the calling God has on our life while on the narrow path.

With the icon-key as a guide, journal the ways you nurture your relationship with the Lord. If that's an area you struggle with, go to Him, and ask Him to help you abide in him, so you can take hold of Him as you run your race.

Nestle

Safety: "If you say, "The Lord is my refuge", and you make the Most High your dwelling, no harm will overtake you, no disaster will come near your tent" Psalm 91:9-10.

Contentment: "Come to me, all you who are weary and burdened, and I will give you rest. Take my yoke upon you and learn from me, for I am gentle and humble in heart, and you will find rest for your souls. For my yoke is easy and my burden is light" Matthew 11:28-30.

Future Hope: "The Lord your God is with you, the Mighty Warrior who saves. He will take great delight in you; in his love he will no longer rebuke you, but will rejoice over you with singing" Zephaniah 3:17. "But now, Lord, what do I look for? My hope is in you" Psalm 29:7.

Isn't it something to think about—the God of all creation, heaven, and earth will rejoice over His people with singing? He will wipe every tear from our eyes! Our hope is in Him alone! Oh, how truly lost I would have been if I had not *held fast* to hope. If not for the Holy Spirit, all hope would have been lost. I thank Him and praise Him that though I had fallen into the pit, He never left me, nor had he forsaken me.

The word *Nestle* brings to my mind something akin to snuggle. I don't think it would be blasphemy to say because of Christ; we can snuggle under the protective *wings* of our Father in Heaven. Our earthly father may have been a perfect example or not a good one at all. Our Heavenly Father is perfect in every way. We can nestle close and feel safe.

He perfectly provides for our every need, both physical and spiritual. He knows we are burdened by our own sin; our

own choices. For our sakes, the Savior took on Himself the burden of our guilt and shame, so we could find contentment and rest in Him.

Meditate on the scripture above. Then read Psalm 91. My friend, do you know the safety of the Lord; the contentment and future hope of a life that's God-connected and directed by Him? If not, do you know why? Write your impressions according to the icon-key.

{T}

TRUTH, TRUST, & TRANSFORMATION

Now, we've come to the crux of our Pivot Point™. It's probably safe to assume life hasn't exactly been a bowl of cherries for you. Maybe circumstances have changed along the way, but the story hasn't. Attempts at a *do-over* haven't turned out so well because—let's face it—we all tend to get stuck handling life the same way we always have.

We get stuck in something like a traffic circle. Here's the thing: *Decide* you're ready to get off the roundabout. That's your Pivot Point™. Next, get yourself fully connected to the Lord. As you begin to know Him better—or maybe for the first time—you'll be able to trust Him for who He is and know who you are in Him. You'll find you're God-directed as you go. Your life begins to take on new purpose and meaning. It sounds trite, but it's true.

Consider *Truth, Trust, and Transformation.* Truth is worth mentioning twice in this book, as well as transformation. Knowing the truth of God is paramount to our faith. Confidence in His truth brings you to a place of trust; another essential. They are the *most* critical steps toward transformational God-connected & directed living.

Truth

Us: "So God created mankind in his own image, in the image of God he created them; male and female he created them" Genesis 1:27. "There is no one righteous, not even one; there is no one who understands; there is no one who seeks God" Romans 3:10-12.

God: "But God demonstrates his own love for us in this: While we were still sinners, Christ died for us" Romans 5:8. "For the wages of sin is death, but the gift of God is eternal life in Christ Jesus our Lord" Romans 6:23. Holy, holy, holy is the Lord God Almighty, who was, and is, and is to come" Revelation 4:8.

In Christ: "to those who believed in his name, he gave the right to become children of God—children born not of natural descent, nor of human decision or a husband's will, but born of God" John 1:12-13. "Now you are the body of Christ, and each one of you is a part of it" 1 Corinthians 12 27. "Since then, you have been raised with Christ, set your hearts on things above, where Christ is, seated at the right hand of God. For you died, and your life is now hidden with Christ in God" Colossians 3:1-3.

We are image-bearers of the Almighty, Triune God. Yet, we choose to go after our own, rather than the will of Him who made us. Consider that carefully. God is a Holy God, and in Him, no evil exists, nor can it reside where He does. Even so, He had mercy on us, Himself paying the death-penalty we deserve. Who can fathom it?

You likely know these things and just as probably have been baptized as a believer in Jesus. Still, you and I live in this

world. While remaining in our *earthly tent,* we are clothed with the righteousness of Christ. Our former selves were crucified with Christ, and yet, like Paul, we do those things we don't want to do, but not the good we desire to do.

When we acknowledge the sovereignty of God—when we get God-connected and directed—living accordingly, our lives are *Transformed.* Instead, we often put ourselves in God's place. This really messes us up, doesn't it? I know this has been true for me. Not that we go around announcing we're our own God, but we sure as heck act like it, don't we? Don't feel singled out, dear friend. I battle this too! I'm so thankful for His grace, aren't you? His mercies are new each day!

Consider the scriptures above; look for more regarding the character of God. With the icon-key as a guide, journal any new insights along with your prayers of confession and thanksgiving.

Trust

Worthy: "Great is the Lord and most worthy of praise; his greatness no one can fathom" Psalm 145:3. "You are worthy, our Lord and God, to receive glory and honor and power, for you created all things, and by your will they were created and have their being" Revelation 4:11.

Faithful: "For I am convinced that neither death nor life, neither angels nor demons, neither the present nor the future, nor any powers, neither height nor depth, nor anything else in all creation, will be able to separate us from the love of God that is in Christ Jesus our Lord" Romans 8:38. May God himself, the God of peace, sanctify you through and through…The one who calls you is faithful, and he will do it" 1 Thessalonians 5:23-24.

Redeemer: "I have swept away your offenses like a cloud, your sins like the morning mist. Return to me, for I have redeemed you" Isaiah 44:22. "Here is a trustworthy saying that deserves full acceptance: Christ Jesus came into the world to save sinners—of whom I am the worst" 1 Timothy 1:15.

Jesus, Jesus, how I trust him! How I've proved him o'er and o'er! Jesus, Jesus, precious Jesus! O for grace to trust him more! Remember that sweet old hymn? Written in 1882, by Louisa M. R. Stead, It reminds me of childhood Sundays.

Admittedly, that song hasn't always rung true for me. I've let that deceiver 'of old' beguile me—not with money or Instagram followers. No, it was with mistrust in God. He's been toying with us this way since the beginning. He's a liar.

God is trustworthy. He's proven His trustworthiness throughout history. He's proven it in our personal history too, hasn't He? *"How I've proved him o'er and o'er!"* Yes, we know this truth. That's not blind faith. That's proof positive!

The Good News of Jesus Christ is that He gave up His rightful place with God to lower Himself, coming to us in human form. He lived sinless, according to the law. He was subjected to every temptation, humiliation, and mutilation any person could ever experience. He was brutally killed and buried. But God would not suffer His son to remain in the pit of death. By the power He already possessed, He rose from the grave, returning to His rightful place at the right hand of the Father.

"Do not let your hearts be troubled. You believe in God; believe also in me. My Father's house has many rooms; if that were not so, would I have told you that I am going there to prepare a place for you? And if I go and prepare a place for you, I will come back and take you to be with me that you also may be where I am. You know the way to the place where I am going" John 14:1-4.

Can you and I put our trust in our Heavenly Father, Christ Jesus, and the Holy Spirit? Yes, we can! It's a choice we make. Every day, make a pivot from our plan to His.

With the icon-key as a guide, journal all of the ways God has proven Himself trustworthy in your life.

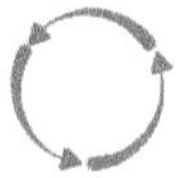

Transformation

Changing: "Do not conform to the pattern of this world, but be transformed by the renewing of your mind. Then you will be able to test and approve what God's will is—his good, pleasing and perfect will" Romans 12:2.

Growing: "Therefore let us move beyond the elementary teachings about Christ and be taken forward to maturity, not laying again the foundation of repentance from acts that lead to death, and of faith in God," Hebrews 6:1. "When I was a child, I talked like a child, I thought like a child, I reasoned like a child. When I became a man, I put the ways of childhood behind me. For now we see only a reflection as in a mirror; then we shall see face to face. Now I know in part; then I shall know fully, even as I am fully known" 1 Corinthians 13:11-12.

Serving: "You, my brothers and sisters, were called to be free. But do not use your freedom to indulge the flesh ; rather, serve one another humbly in love" Galatians 5:13. "Each of you should use whatever gift you have received to serve others, as faithful stewards of God's grace in its various forms" 1 Peter 4:10. "In the same way, let your light shine before others, that they may see your good deeds and glorify your Father in heaven" Matthew 5:16.

Transformation takes time. Some, like me, take more time! When we first surrender ourselves to God, it's true that we are made into a new creation; in an instant. However, sanctification—becoming more and more like Christ—is a process moved along by the Holy Spirit.

Many of us have had some *rough* bumps and bruises—perhaps deeper wounds than that. Early on, we may have heard

a voice whisper to us, *unworthy* or *unlovable*, even *you don't belong*. I've heard all three. At various times, I've let that voice rule my life. I've gone into the pit of darkness. I've tasted despair. I've blindly indulged where we're never meant to go.

As much as it feels right to say, "It wasn't your fault," to be a victim or feel justified in your wrong actions; it was a choice. We've been given that choice by our Creator. Choose life, or choose death. That may sound harsh, but it's true. Remaining a victim is death. Dwelling in our own counsel is death.

As a life-long believer in Christ, I should have chosen to surrender long ago. I can tell you as soon as I began to cry out to God for *His* understanding, the change inside was palpable to me. It was gradual. Little by little, I felt Him wash over and through me. I began to choose each day to leave behind the me-cycle and work on getting my life God-connected & directed.

Have I *made it* yet? Nope! I have to work out my faith daily. So do you. Living in faith is sometimes hard, but the yoke of Christ is so much lighter than the oppression of the enemy.

Choose transformation, my friend! Step into your Christ-bought, God-given privilege to walk in His Way. He is faithful! Journal how the Lord is transforming you, according to the icon-key.

PIVOT POINT

CONCLUSION

What Then, Shall We Do?

Let's stop eating only cake and join the Lord at His abundant table instead. Let's make a pivot. Let's make the *glory of God,* and His love become the point of our lives. Let's become anchored by the deep, abiding faith we need to weather the storms of this life.

Let's live realizing that faith isn't a magic pill that either works or doesn't. Instead, faith is something that we work out in our lives as evidence of our salvation. We can lay down our grief, disappointment, betrayals, and even our own bad choices at the foot of the cross, for He is worthy of our confidence and trust. He is faithful to see us through it.

We can have confidence in His infinite mercy, patience, and grace, as He lovingly meets us in the midst of our mess. Let's not treat Jesus as if we have Him at the ready in our back pocket. He has said about Himself, "I AM."

Let us get more connected to God as we remain in the Word. Let us gain a deeper understanding of the Trinity and who *we* are in relation to a Holy God. As we do this, He has promised to direct our paths. Let us make a pivot—changing our minds, changing the direction we've been traveling, living our lives indeed transformed, and full of the love of the Lord.

What then, shall we do? We allow the transformational love of God to penetrate all that we are. We go out to the world, giving the love we've received, changing lives as we do. *Changed lives, change lives.* It's God who does the heart-work, but He chooses *us* to do the leg-work.

Yes, He loves us faithfully. Yes, in Christ, we are worthy! Yes, there is now no condemnation for those in Christ Jesus!

You are fearfully and wonderfully made and beautiful in your time. Stand tall and confident in the Lord. Give love because you are loved.

Who deserves all of the glory for this? He does! Make today your Pivot Point™, my sister. Change your mind. Change direction. Be transformed, shining light and love to a darkened world! *It's the secret to everything.*

"Day and night they never stop saying: 'Holy, holy, holy is the Lord God Almighty,' who was, and is, and is to come'" Revelation 4:8.

For His glory-
Grace and Peace,

Lori Ann Thompson

Lori Ann Thompson

> "Now to him who is able to do immeasurably more than all we ask or imagine, according to his power that is at work within us, to him be glory in the church and in Christ Jesus throughout all generations, for ever and ever! Amen" Ephesians 3:20-21.

Let's do this together!

You don't have to go it alone on this journey!
Connect with me for:

- Individual Coaching
- Private Group Coaching
- Future Limited Group Retreats

the road ahead

Is waiting for you!

lori@loriannthompson.com
@heyitsme_lori
https://loriannthompson.com
https://www.facebook.com/Author.LoriAThompson